"Jeff Tacklind is a surprising and winsome voice with a wide reach. He writes with the vulnerability of someone who just wants to be a little more like Jesus. But behind his easygoing tone you'll find the riches of a seasoned spiritual director and pastor."

Ian Morgan Cron, author of *The Road Back to You*

"*The Winding Path of Transformation* is so unique, so vulnerable, so reflective that it is hard to find words to do it justice. Written like a novel and drawing from sources as different as Kierkegaard and Cyndi Lauper, Tacklind's work is, at once, deeply personal and also an insightful, helpful depiction of the shared contours of every person's pilgrimage. Deep, authentic, wise, and hopeful, *The Winding Path of Transformation* is a rich guide for all who hunger for a more deeply transformed life."

J. P. Moreland, distinguished professor of philosophy, Talbot School of Theology, Biola University, author of *Finding Quiet*

"Very few authors could summon the courage to write this book. But be warned: it takes almost as much courage to read this book as it took to write it. If you go down this yellow winding road with the author, you will move around the entire color wheel of emotions. You will gasp at its honesty; you will squirm and wince and feel uncomfortable at its vulnerability; you will shake your head in marvel and wonderment at its revelations; you will cry. But the promise of the title is real—your own story journey will be transformed."

Leonard Sweet, author, Charles Wesley Professor of Doctoral Studies at Evangelical Seminary, founder of preachthestory.com

"As a young Christian, I imagined what it would look like to mature in my faith. Looking back now, I realize the path was far more winding than I could have anticipated. I appreciate Jeff's life-tested and pastorally wise counsel in *The Winding Path of Transformation*. It's a wonderful guide along the path of growth."

Alan Fadling, president of Unhurried Living Inc.

"I love this quiet, deeply honest book; it indeed has left me—as the author hopes will be the case for his readers—with a renewed appetite for transformation and freedom and an awareness of God's presence, 'Always already.'"

Jennifer Grant, author of *Love You More* and *Maybe God Is like That Too*

"Oh, how I have wished that transformation could come through reading a book. Jeff addresses this fallacy head-on. Transformation comes through opening up the fodder of our lives to the slow work of God. Period. Jeff gently coaxes us to stand in the places of engagement, where we live deeply out of our own skin, away from the shallow shoulds and into the sacred invitation imprinted on our souls. I am grateful to have such a holy and humble traveling companion in this beautiful book."

Beth Slevcove, author of *Broken Hallelujahs: Learning to Grieve the Big and Small Losses of Life*

FOREWORD BY
CATHLEEN FALSANI

JEFFREY TACKLIND

THE
WINDING
PATH OF
TRANSFORMATION

FINDING YOURSELF BETWEEN
GLORY AND HUMILITY

An imprint of InterVarsity Press
Downers Grove, Illinois

InterVarsity Press
P.O. Box 1400, Downers Grove, IL 60515-1426
ivpress.com
email@ivpress.com

InterVarsity Press® is the book-publishing division of InterVarsity Christian Fellowship/USA®, a movement of students and faculty active on campus at hundreds of universities, colleges, and schools of nursing in the United States of America, and a member movement of the International Fellowship of Evangelical Students. For information about local and regional activities, visit intervarsity.org.

All Scripture quotations, unless otherwise indicated, are taken from The Holy Bible, New International Version®, NIV®. Copyright © 1973, 1978, 1984, 2011 by Biblica, Inc.™ Used by permission of Zondervan. All rights reserved worldwide. www.zondervan.com. The "NIV" and "New International Version" are trademarks registered in the United States Patent and Trademark Office by Biblica, Inc.™

While any stories in this book are true, some names and identifying information may have been changed to protect the privacy of individuals.

Cover design and image composite: David Fassett
Interior design: Jeanna Wiggins

ISBN 978-0-8308-4650-4 (print)
ISBN 978-0-8308-7224-4 (digital)

Printed in the United States of America ⊗

Library of Congress Cataloging-in-Publication Data
Names: Tacklind, Jeff, 1971- author.
Title: The winding path of transformation : finding yourself between glory and humility / Jeff Tacklind.
Description: Downers Grove, IL : IVP Books, [2019].
Identifiers: LCCN 2019013105 (print) | LCCN 2019015971 (ebook) | ISBN 9780830872244 (eBook) | ISBN 9780830846504 (pbk. : alk. paper) | ISBN 9780830872244 (ebk.)
Subjects: LCSH: Spiritual life—Christianity. | Christian life.
Classification: LCC BV4501.3 (ebook) | LCC BV4501.3 .T265 2019 (print) | DDC 248.4—dc23
LC record available at https://lccn.loc.gov/2019013105

P	20	19	18	17	16	15	14	13	12	11	10	9	8	7	6	5	4	3	2	1
Y	36	35	34	33	32	31	30	29	28	27	26	25	24	23	22	21	20	19		

To Patty

CONTENTS

FOREWORD

Cathleen Falsani

SUNDAY, MAY 16, 2010.

That was the day Jeff Tacklind delivered the best sermon I've ever heard. Before or since.

The Best. Period. Full stop. And I say that as someone who, as a religion journalist, has gone to church for a living for a couple of decades and has been "churched" in one Christian tradition or another from the day I was born. Homiletics (AKA *preachin'*) is my baseball.

His message that morning, exegeting the fourth chapter of the book of Job from Hebrew Scripture, was a humdinger. Humble, funny, literate, astute, accessible, compassionate, vulnerable, and profoundly, achingly honest. Quintessential Jeff, really.

What Jeff taught that morning from the pulpit of Little Church by the Sea—swathed in an overgrown cardigan, hand-thrown pottery mug in one hand, floppy Bible in the other—continues to reverberate through my spirit nearly a decade since, as I suspect it will for the rest of my time on this side of the eternal veil. It recalibrated the way I see my life and understand my story—the one God is writing and the arc of which I get only the most fleeting of occasional glimpses usually while jubilating on a proverbial mountaintop or wallowing in a slough of despond.

What Jeff explained so tenderly is that we are not the ones writing the story of our lives. That task belongs solely to the God of grace who knows how it begins and how it ends and is intimately familiar with (and present in) the vast middle, where all of us mere mortals dwell (and the immortal, living God dwells with us).

Toward the end of his message, Jeff read a passage from Sue Monk Kidd's *When the Heart Waits: Spiritual Direction for Life's Sacred Questions,* where she says: "We seem to have focused so much on exuberant beginnings and victorious endings that we've forgotten about the slow, sometimes torturous unraveling of God's grace that takes place in the 'middle places.'"

Sometimes the middle place is also a liminal space—a threshold where we abide between one chapter, reality, or iteration of ourselves, and whatever comes next. The morning Jeff preached on Job 4, I was waiting nervously in a liminal space that felt much more like an iron maiden than a doorway. There was an adoption hearing scheduled for early June 2010 in Malawi, our son's birthplace, and a week later we would fly to the other side of the world to meet the African judge who would decide whether we would return to California as a forever family, or not.

This was the summer that the volcano in Iceland kept erupting, disrupting air travel in Europe (and in turn elsewhere) on and off for weeks. We could not be late for or, God forbid, miss the hearing we'd been waiting on tenterhooks for months to be scheduled, so with just two-weeks' notice, we had to figure out how to get from southern California to southern Africa while avoiding the Icelandic volcano. No pressure.

As I sat in the pew in Little Church, about to embark on a literal epic journey into an unknown where the outcome was now entirely out of my control (not that it ever was within *my* control in the first place), waves of terror had me attempting to white-knuckle drive the narrative. Would it hold? Was the story a comedy (of errors or otherwise)? A tragedy, a thriller, or a dreaded cliffhanger?

The torturous unraveling of God's grace, indeed.

But here's the thing: in his Job sermon, Jeff assured me that I wasn't alone while I waited for the answers, for the moment when the divine drone rises above the tree line and the camera reveals the perspective from one thousand feet. The wide shot. The bigger picture. Even for a few seconds.

God is with us in the tension of our middle places. Always present, even when we feel like God's left the building and is, as a buddy of ours likes to say, "Down at the pub having a pint." God walks with us along the winding road, when we don't know where we're headed. God sits next to us on the rock when we're lost in a wood, and strides a few yards ahead of us in the stream showing us where to step to make a way through or where to plant our feet and bend with the current as the waters move past us.

Jeff preached a message that widened the aperture of my heart and gave me a new lens through which to see my story, accumulating hard-won wisdom and experience of middle places—those quotidian plateaus between the thrill of victory and the agony of defeat; the sweeping prairies and pasturelands of uncertainty that connect glory to humility and hold them in active tension.

Jeff has collected what he has learned like a basket of polished river stones in this winsome and welcoming volume of stories not as an expert, but as a humble fellow pilgrim on the way. He doesn't have it all figured out and he doesn't pretend that he does. He's got a brilliant mind that is eclipsed only by his humble spirit. He has listened for and heard God's voice in the actual wilderness and inside the walls of an art museum, in wild goose chases and the words of a charismatic prophet; in the "book of nature," volumes of poetry, *The Lord of the Rings*, the collected works of Clive Staples Lewis, St. Thérèse of Lisieux's "little way," and the lineup at Trestles. He has encountered God in the wild eyes of a stranger, the upturned gaze of Christ crucified, the faces of his children, and the arms of his beloved.

Jeff was my friend long before he was my pastor. He was one of the first people I met when we visited Laguna Beach from Chicago for the first time, when the idea of living in a sleepy Southern California surf town wasn't even a distant glimmer in our imagination.

I immediately liked and trusted Jeff—no easy feat for someone whose vocational mantra is "if your mother says she loves you, check it out." And he has never, not for a moment, given me cause to second-guess my first impressions of him. I tell you this, dear reader, because you can trust him too.

Much of the time I call him "Rabbi," because he reminds me of Jewish clergy friends who are more interested in helping people ask questions than they are in dispensing definitive answers—a trait I've found to be less common among the professional Christians I've met. Perhaps it's because one of the things he's learned during various sojourns in his middle places is that God knows us waaaaaaay better than we even know ourselves. There's no point in pretending. To be known like that, he says, is a powerful and vulnerable gift.

Jeff is neither threatened by nor afraid of doubt. But he is deeply skeptical of certainty. If he doesn't know something, he'll happily admit it, and he does more than a few times in the pages that follow herein.

"God's riddles," Jeff says, "take us on a journey. He leads us with such patience and care, step by step, often silent, but always there."

Jeff will be your trail guide for the upcoming tour of middle places. Pace yourself. Slow down. Savor it. Stretch. Stay hydrated.

There are no stupid questions.

And remember: *Not all those who wander are lost* . . .

PREFACE

Consider what God has done:
Who can straighten
what he has made crooked?

ECCLESIASTES 7:13

THIS BOOK IS ABOUT TRANSFORMATION . . . about doing deep heart work. It's about discovering interior freedom and seeing God's masterful hand at work. And it is about glory and humility and the beautiful way they interact to drive us toward our true selves. Even when the way appears crooked and bent. Even when the path turns unexpectedly. Especially when it does.

But transformation isn't merely the subject matter being discussed. The truths of this work are woven into the fabric of the writing itself. Because writing this book was a bit of a crooked journey. A winding path. And it continues to speak deep truths into my life to this very day.

The writing process was much more discovery than deduction. It emerged rather than having been constructed. And the ideas that I share are both as truthful and as raw as I felt I could be. That means I'm still wrestling and grappling with them. The stories I've written are continuing to shape me, and I'm still mining their depths. It continues to be a work in progress, as do I, one that I trust will never be finished, at least not in this life.

Carl Rogers said, "What is the most personal is the most universal." I'm banking on that. That these words I've written and stories of transformation wouldn't merely illuminate the details of my own journey, but would cast vision for yours. That they would create a lens through which to clarify your own moments of consolation and desolation, and that you too might better recognize the subtle hand of God at work in your own story.

Because life is a winding road. Unpredictable. Confusing. And without a clear course or map. And this winding seems to be intentional—it's there by design. It ensures that we remain close and pay attention to our guide, and learn to trust his words even when times are cold and dark, or when the voice has become quiet or even absent. When we start to lose our vision, and begin to long for the comforts of home.

And the winding path ensures that our eyes become trained to see and recognize the provision and goodness that otherwise go overlooked in our hurry to get from one place to the next. Because these glimpses of joy along the path sustain us. They renew us. And they remind us that there is more to come.

Because our hearts long for more. At least mine does. And I hope yours does too. And as you read, I hope that your appetite for transformation and freedom would increase. That you would learn to walk in deeper faith through the paradoxes and complexities of life. And that, in the midst of life's tension, you would learn to walk with courage down this winding path of transformation that leads ultimately to glory.

PART 1

GLORY AND HUMILITY

Ever since I was a child, I've longed to live a life of nobility and glory. In every adventure story I was caught up in, or hero's biography I digested, there was the underlying question: *Could this be me?* I longed to live a glorious story. But this longing has always been held in check by a more cautious, but no less virtuous voice, telling me to beware my pride and self-conceit—that part of me that would quickly rise up in moments of triumph and contaminate them with my own fantasies and self-indulgence and aggrandizement. These two longings have forever created tension in the deepest places of my heart. A battle for both glory and humility.

At first these longings appeared to be at odds. Like a continuum where balance looked like a compromise between the two, where character and wisdom existed at the midpoint of the spectrum. My initial assumption looks something like this.

GLORY | HUMILITY

But this has proven to be a huge distortion of the truth. It leads to a small story. It leads to comfort over risk and insecurity over glory. In my stories that I've written, I've seen how God is asking me not to compromise the two, but instead is asking for more of both. To live a life simultaneously full of glory *and* humility. He won't settle for less. And neither should I. In this view, glory and humility are no longer on opposite ends of the spectrum. Instead, they are two different trajectories, separate spectrums that intersect.

And this creates its own tension and pull. But instead of pulling us in opposite directions, they create a new trajectory. Glory and humility are vectors and we are being pulled by the two forces toward a new path. Toward what I've called transformation.

But transformation is far from a simple linear path. The tension this creates can feel exhausting. At times it feels confusing or even misleading. Glory and humility can feel almost self-contradictory.

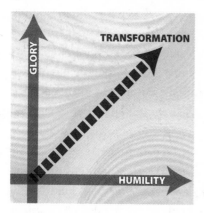

But as I've been learning to hold both with open hands, I'm seeing a thread emerge, a leading toward greater freedom and wholeness. I hope that, as you follow this journey with me, you will start to discover this thread, this pattern in your own life. And that you'll savor the tension for the unique invitation it brings.

1

AT HOME IN
THE MIDDLE PLACE

A FEW MONTHS AGO, I WAS WALKING in Mill Creek Canyon when I heard God's voice. I had been given an assignment: find a symbol in nature that spoke to me of my current spiritual state. As I got up and began to head out the door of the cabin and into the rocky streambed, I have to admit it was with some foot-dragging.

As a pastor, I have seen the value of such experiential exercises, and I've led plenty myself. But I've never liked having to participate in them. As I began to walk, I already had decided how I would complete the task with both an object and explanation that would be sufficient to share with the group.

That might sound more cynical than I intend. It wasn't unbelief that left me resigned to simply completing the task. I was exhausted. Ministry and life had been taking a toll on my heart. With reluctance I strode out into the canyon, my heart empty, my ears closed, and my eyes looking downward to keep from stumbling.

Someone once asked me how I, personally, recognize the voice of God.

How do I distinguish between the divine whisper and my own wishful or sometimes fearful thinking? Is there really a difference?

A fair question.

I've noticed from time to time that God's voice and mine do have similarities in tone. Often I mistake them at first, God's words as my own. But, in the end, I'm learning that there is a distinct difference. God's words seem to enter my mind from my peripheral vision. They present themselves—unlooked for—and they take me by surprise.

As I considered how to respond to the question, the word that came immediately to mind was *resistance*. When I hear God speak, it's rarely what I'm hoping to hear. My ego flares. I feel defensive, self-protective, and guarded.

Often I'm disappointed because my agenda feels hijacked, my plans are interrupted, and my ambitions cast aside. There is an uncomfortable, even invasive, truthfulness to the words, opening doors I'd rather remain closed, and taking me places I'd rather not go. God's voice asks more of me than I desire to give.

But that's not all I feel. Almost as strong as my resistance and disappointment is a paradoxical leap of the heart. That small, true self steps forward from the shadows with longing and hope. In a burst of courage, childlike dreams emerge and reawaken.

God is here. We are on holy ground.

As I walked along the rocky middle ground of Mill Creek, I became aware of the opposing cliffs rising steeply on either side of me. The creek runs almost perfectly east to west, resulting in two very different ecosystems on the north and south sides. The north-facing side remains predominantly shaded and therefore is covered with evergreens, mainly ponderosa pines and incense cedars. On the other side of the canyon—the sunny side—there are oaks, manzanitas, and even cacti. Two very different worlds carved in half by a meandering stream and barren quarry.

The creek bed was wide, disproportionately so. The creek itself was maybe five feet across, while the creek bed was probably two hundred.

The banks rose at least fifteen or twenty feet on each side. You'd never guess that much water could fill this valley bank to bank, but I've seen it happen. Sometimes years go by without a flash flood, but when it comes the creek is transformed into a raging torrent. Boulders the size of cars go thundering along, tossed about with ease. The power of those floods is both captivating and terrifying.

But most days it looks just like this. A meandering brook. A quiet, still, middle place separating two very different worlds.

Back home, I am the pastor of a small church in Laguna Beach, California. It's an eclectic and eccentric, diverse and charming faith community. It also is quirky, difficult, reactive, and dysfunctional—just as all churches are to one extent or another. Our church comprises people from many different Christian tribes, from Pentecostals, staunch fundamentalists and contemplatives, to charismatics, traditionalists, and progressives. We have people who regularly speak in tongues, and others who believe such spiritual displays are a bunch of nonsense.

We hang in there, like families do. And we continue, together, to hold. To me, that alone is evidence of God's grace.

The church itself wasn't the source of my exhaustion. I was.

Standing in the threshold of midlife, with the repetitiveness of fourteen years invested in one place and the vast rest of my life bearing down on me, I was holding steady, but my fingers were starting to cramp. I felt like I was constantly being buffeted and worn down. So on my scavenger hunt for a totem to represent my torpor, I decided to pick up a smooth stone from the creek bed. I could spin that in a positive direction. Something about how God was removing my abrasive exterior, and, over time, polishing me into something beautiful.

It was true enough. I knew that God was with me in my struggle. But this is what happens when ministry becomes vocation. It becomes your job to produce insightful metaphors and images and to share them with just the right amount of vulnerability and humility. It becomes rote. It becomes disengaged from the heart.

The truth was, I was lonely. I still am. Deep down I just wanted to belong instead of constantly finding myself somewhere in the middle.

My name—Jeffrey—means "peacemaker." But for many years my parents felt they'd misnamed me. I'm a questioner, maybe to a fault. I never could let ideas just be. I picked at them and turned them upside down. It was curiosity and a need to understand, at least at its best. But I had a tendency to wear out the patience of my teachers and instructors and friends.

Over the years, I was learning that this quality was suited to finding the truth in the middle of things. In philosophy, this is referred to as the via media. It is a middle way or compromise between extremes. For some reason, this is always where I ended up. In between views. Seeing the value in both sides but not entirely convinced by either. I've learned that this is a lonely place to live, but that it carries with it a unique value.

Most people are largely unaware that they have a bias. It is therefore helpful to have an objective, questioning voice in the discussion, leading opposing sides to a kind of reconciliation or compromise. This is a form of peacemaking. But I've also seen that the resolution it creates never is quite enough to completely satisfy either side, equally pleasing and displeasing to both parties. It leaves the peacemaker alone at the center—with a foot in both camps—belonging to neither.

As I walked the middle place of the creek, stumbling from rock to rock, my heart felt as dry as the mounds of sand and quartz. I surveyed the different worlds on either side of me, realizing my deep yearning to belong somewhere—to pick a side and sink my roots there. To escape this middle ground. To settle into that place of comfortable orthodoxy. To stop asking questions. To stop seeing the value in the opposing arguments. To stop listening with empathy to the other side.

As a pastor, I'm often asked to weigh in on matters of controversy and confusion. One such issue recently had arisen in my church and congregants were desperate for me to state clearly my own position. They wanted to know where I stood, but weren't particularly interested in my insight or perspective. The underlying question was a form of "are you with me, or against me?"

Often, in moments such as these, my go-to defense is to stand behind a recognized outside authority. C. S. Lewis is my go-to. Very few people are willing to write him off, and he, better than anyone I have read, has navigated the middle places of theology with grace and aplomb. But in this case, I felt I was on new ground, on my own. With all the personal integrity I could muster, I simply stated, "It's complicated." I said more words than that, but, in the end, that was the gist. My answer pleased no one and seemed to disappoint everyone.

Dallas Willard wrote about peacemakers in *The Divine Conspiracy*. He was discussing an alternative reading of the Beatitudes, where "blessed are" instead is translated "blessed even are." He goes through each of the Beatitudes verse by verse. When he gets to peacemakers he has this to say:

> They make the list because outside the kingdom they are, as is often said, "called everything but a child of God." That is because they are always in the middle. [Ask the policeman called in to smooth out a domestic dispute. There is no situation more dangerous.] Neither side trusts you. Because they know that you are looking at both sides, you can't possibly be on their side.

The matter I was struggling with hardly would qualify as a police dispute, but it was certainly domestic. These were my people, my family. We are a small church. Any split or tear draws blood. As fear and even suspicion replaced a look of trust in the eyes, the pain I felt wasn't simply a need to belong. Part of it was the despair that comes from watching two opposing sides completely miss each other in the discussion. Members of each side hold fast to a cherished value that they have built into a fortified position that members of the other side fail to see because they are too busy constructing and defending their own position and argument. An almighty disconnect is the end result when logical trajectories never seem to intersect with each other, except to criticize and reject one another as they go flying past.

Alasdair MacIntyre used the metaphor of a map in his book *After Virtue*. Each of us holds pieces of a map, the entirety of which has been destroyed. All that we have left are fragments with no way of connecting them together. There often seems to be no hope of recovering the larger meaning or *telos,* as he calls it. This system is damaged irreparably.

When I have this feeling of despair, it is hard to shake. Things feel stuck, helpless. I don't know where to begin. I'm at the end of my rope.

It is always at this very point that I am tempted to give in and placate. I compromise my position and move towards the more conservative side of my upbringing. This might even appear to be something like wisdom, but really, deep down, it is more of a wanting to fit in somewhere I know I don't fully belong. It might last for a brief season, but it never provides what my heart longs for most deeply: true belonging and unconditional love that isn't based on how I performed (or didn't) on any given Sunday.

There is an image in Scripture that I always have found moving. It comes from the book of Isaiah where it says,

They will be called oaks of righteousness,
> a planting of the LORD
> for the display of his splendor." (Isaiah 61:3)

How I long to be that righteous oak, with roots spread wide. Strong and resilient. Enduring through the years. Trustworthy.

And then I heard God speak to me in that lonely middle place. God simply said, "This is who you are." I looked up and in front of me was this thin, white tree, standing alone in the midst of the creek bed. A white alder. It caught me off guard.

This *tree? This unimpressive, wan, frail-looking specimen?*

My heart pushed back, resisting the image and the calling that came with it. It wasn't just the tree itself that made me withdraw, but where it grew, this rocky middle place. To sink roots here was to plant myself in the place of loneliness. Something in me writhed in protest, refusing to go quietly.

I realized that one of the things that kept me going, even when I felt exhausted, was the temporality of my current calling. This middle place I presently inhabited was a season, a chapter, which soon would pass. That my identity and calling should be symbolized by a white alder burst that illusion of temporality, this dream of picking a side on which to belong and joining it permanently. Because I knew something about this tree. For one thing, it cannot survive anywhere except here, in the creek bed. It requires too much water to live anywhere else. This is its weakness. It is so dependent on a constant water supply that it withers as it moves farther away from its source of nourishment.

It cannot leave the river and hope to survive. It is too thirsty.

And yet, the white alder alone remains in this barren space. This is because of several unique strengths the tree possesses that allow

it to endure where other trees are uprooted and perish. For one, it
is incredibly flexible. When the floods come, it concedes. It bends,
sometimes completely over, only to straighten again as the torrent
subsides. Everything else in the path of the flood is stripped away
as the deluge of water rises bank to bank. The larger oak is incapable
of bending. Even a strong wind can break off its large branches,
whereas the saturated wood of the alder yields.

But it is not simply the pliability of the alder wood that allows it
to remain. Its root system also is distinct. It possesses what is called
a taproot: essentially the trunk of the tree continues to grow down
and down, digging deeper and deeper in its thirst for more of the
water it needs to survive. Not only does the taproot allow the alder
to endure the floods, it also allows the tree to survive when the
creek's water level is at its lowest. Oak and pine trees have breadth
but not necessarily depth. Their shallower root systems cannot
endure the barrenness of the middle place when the soil and nourishment they need have been leached away.

Staring at the lone white alder, I could feel my heart change. The
resistance abided, but as I felt God's demand on my life increasing
beyond my own strength and resources of love and energy, a childlike
leap also arose, fueled by joy that springs from the affirmation only
God can give. It makes me think of God's word to Jeremiah,

> If you have raced with men on foot
>   and they have worn you out,
>   how can you compete with horses?
> If you stumble in safe country,
>   how will you manage in the thickets by the Jordan?
>   (Jeremiah 12:5)

I love that verse, where I hear God saying to his exhausted prophet,
"You're faster than this . . . You are far faster than you can imagine." It
is a huge paradigm shift, calculating our endurance based on resources

beyond ourselves, demonstrating our neediness but also our potential. It is vulnerable, even humbling, but also replete with vision.

And this is where we peacemakers must learn to thrive. It is where our hearts are transformed. As we learn to drink deeply from this river we are changed, and so is the world around us. In Jeremiah 31:2 God says that we will find "favor in the wilderness." The wilderness becomes the place of blessing, of intimacy, and of deepest belonging.

There is a term that has been passed down from Celtic Christianity called a thin place. It is where the distance between heaven and earth becomes paper thin, almost indistinguishable. Sometimes it even intersects. It is the place of the burning bush, the quiet whisper, of visions and dreams. Too easily we can pass by these places and never recognize them. The still, small voice goes unheard. The sacred ground passes quickly beneath our feet. Like Jacob said, "Surely the LORD is in this place, and I was not aware of it." But when we do hear the voice, everything changes. Sometimes these thin places are incredibly beautiful, but often they are not. The desert, at first glance, is barren, rocky, and lifeless. And yet God's presence completely transforms it.

This is the power of hearing the voice of God. To hear it is to begin to understand the love of God. This love is the love of a good father who sees far deeper into us than we can. He knows us better than we know ourselves. Everything else feels like a cheap substitute in comparison. We can do our best to medicate our longings, or we can listen. We can search for intimate connections with others, but we will never be known to the extent that God can and does know us. To know it, we must quiet our hearts and wait for his voice. We must let God's words do their work of transformation, bringing out our true selves and speaking into us our true calling.

I am learning to embrace this calling as peacemaker. Part of me cringes even as I write that. The idea of sinking my roots here in the rocky creek—to be alone, and yet not alone—is intimidating. The invitation comes to sink my roots deep, to let God quench this insatiable thirst for intimacy and connection, to search for him with my whole heart.

This book is about my journey thus far. As I find myself entering the middle stage of my life, I am learning to savor the work that God uniquely does in this liminal space.

It is constantly changing and growing. Each time, a bit of me dies. That place of self-sufficiency. My ego. It withers and in its place, God offers the space for humility to take root. But simultaneously, God also offers glory. He speaks into my life a vision that extends beyond my hopes and dreams.

These two trajectories, I'm realizing, are constantly at work. Having the eyes to see and ears to hear requires intentionality and discernment. But, in the end, the results are life changing. As Paul promises in 1 Corinthians 2:9,

> However, as it is written:
>   "What no eye has seen,
>   what no ear has heard,
>   and what no human mind has conceived"—
>   the things God has prepared for those who love him—

FOR REFLECTION AND CONVERSATION

1. How do you recognize the voice of God in your life?

2. Where does your heart resist God's voice? Where does it leap?

3. Is there a thin place in your life where God's voice is most clear? What does that place tell you about how God sees your heart?

4. Where has your heart been planted? What will it take for you to thrive in the place where God has placed you?

2

GROWING
DEEP ROOTS

I'VE ALWAYS BEEN A RELUCTANT LEADER. When a crisis hits, when a decision has to be made, when action needs to be taken, my knee jerk response is to wait and see if someone else is going to step in. And when they do, I breathe a sigh of relief. Because to take leadership is to take responsibility, and honestly, most times I'd prefer not to.

Instead, I'd rather come alongside whoever is in charge. I prefer to lend my experience or expertise to the situation without having to assume control and take on the responsibility for the outcome. I would prefer to just make a contribution without shouldering the weight of liability.

And yet, leadership is my calling. Authority has been given to me, like a hand-me-down coat that is two sizes too large. It isn't so big that it falls off, but the sleeves extend over my hands. This coat of authority that I wear reveals to me just how much growing I need to do.

When the lead pastor spot opened up at my church, I was the obvious next in line. After all, I was already the copastor with the man who had filled the role for the last twenty years. But my role, if I'm honest, was much more assistant than copastor. Although the tasks and roles I had taken on were significant, and my list of responsibilities was long, the authority piece was his. It couldn't be handed off or even shared. Ultimate authority cannot be delegated.

A friend of mine, who is a basketball coach, told me that the move from assistant coach to head coach is only one chair. It is the smallest move incrementally, and yet everything suddenly looks different. He's right. I don't think you can ever really prepare yourself for that switch. It is something you have to experience for yourself.

As the elder board at my church began the process of considering me for the role of head pastor, not everyone was convinced I was ready. The thought of it caused all my deep insecurities to scream out their accusations: "You aren't ready!" "You don't have what it takes!" "You can't be trusted!" "You are hopelessly flawed!" The fact that they hesitated just confirmed that there were at least elements of truth in my self-doubt.

Even though I agreed with their caution, I was deeply disappointed to witness their hesitancy. How I longed for their confidence to offset my own feelings of inadequacy! I desperately wanted their assured affirmations, that I might be able to believe them myself.

What they did instead was deliberate. They prayed. They wrestled. As, of course, they should have. In my personal fantasies, I'm so gifted that no consideration is necessary. But that is a ridiculous fallacy. And were they not to deliberate, it would have cheapened their final approval. This "being weighed" was necessary. Especially for my own heart.

When we gathered back together, I sat with some trepidation, awaiting their decision. The man with the most hesitancy spoke first. And he said these words . . . familiar words that were already dear to my heart. He said, "God told me that 'Deep roots are not reached by the frost.' I'm convinced now that you are the right person for this role."

Those words took me aback. That line is from a poem that is dear to my heart. The credit for it belongs to J. R. R. Tolkien, from *The Lord of the Rings*, but if you asked me, I'd tell you it was written by Bilbo Baggins. In elvish. About Aragorn. It is more than poetry. It is prophecy.

The poem speaks about Aragorn as the coming king. The first verse says,

> All that is gold does not glitter,
> Not all those who wander are lost;
> The old that is strong does not wither,
> Deep roots are not reached by the frost.

Now, I love Tolkien's *The Lord of the Rings*. I started with *The Hobbit* and the Narnia books when I was young, but progressed to LOTR when my dad would read it to me. It was a bit over my head at the time (all that history and elvish poetry), and it was maybe a little too suspenseful for my ten-year-old emotions at bedtime (black riders chasing Hobbits through Bree kept me up more than once), but I was hooked from day one. I loved the immersive world Tolkien had created, with all the languages, history, races, ages, and depth of mythology. To read Tolkien is to be ushered into a magnificent story, in a world so vast and real that the story itself is a mere glimpse into the greater whole of Middle Earth.

As a child, when I read these stories, something deep in me would stir. Something not only real, but more real, more true than the world around me. I was moved by emotions that were familiar and yet being awakened for the first time. A longing for depth and nobility, for a life of glorious deeds done without need of recognition, and for depth of character that refused to turn back or look away in despair when hope was seemingly lost.

As I would read, I would find myself desiring to be the very best version of myself. Because I see in the characters not only characteristics I long to possess but a quality of life that feels big enough to contain my heart. Something about the mythical and heroic speaks to our truest callings in life. And that calling is glory. Not fame. Not success. But glory.

The Hebrew word *kavod* captures it best. It means "weighty." Solid. Heavy. We are made to live lives that are big enough for eternity. To walk in a manner that the world is not worthy of.

As I heard those words spoken over me—"Deep roots are not reached by the frost"—in that upper room in my church, I felt my heart leap. I knew I would never be the type A, confident and bold leader that others wanted me to be. That has never been my trajectory. But a leader like Aragorn, humble, reluctant, a fighter, but without the need for the crown. Could I be like that? I didn't know. But I did know one thing . . . I wanted to be. I wanted to be that kind of man.

I think callings have this way of addressing both longings and fears at the same time. It's another one of those intersections we come to in life. We can trust the callings that speak not only to our gifts, but to our fears. And while this might seem obvious, it certainly isn't natural. Instead we prefer roles in which we will shine. We play to our strengths. But true calling has a much longer trajectory. It shows us who we are becoming. Who we already are in God's eyes.

There is a wonderful story about a man named Gideon in the book of Judges. An angel appears to him while he is hiding in the bottom of a well threshing his wheat. Threshing requires wind, and the bottom of a well is probably the least effective location to perform this task. But it was preferable to Gideon because he was terrified of being spotted by his enemies.

An angel appears to Gideon in this place of trepidation and when the angel addresses him, he calls him "mighty warrior." This might have an angelic tone of sarcasm to it, I don't know. But the fact is, it is a name that foreshadows Gideon's destiny. It is the description of who he will become. And in the angelic realm, it is who he already is.

I can relate to Gideon's fear. When I feel cautious or insecure, I detach. I hide. But God has this way of chasing me to those lonely, hiding places. Of speaking into my fragility words that capture my heart and fill me with hope and vision.

"Deep roots are not reached by the frost." That line wasn't just a word of affirmation from an older friend. It wasn't just a nudge toward where God was leading me. It was filled with wise counsel. "Jeff, you must grow deeper roots." That's what I heard. And that is what I long to do.

Deep roots . . . like the alder. A taproot that gives stability, ensures nourishment, and allows for the tree to endure the harsh winters. Without depth, the tree will perish from the cold.

But trees don't just naturally sink their roots deep. They do so as they search for water. I learned that from the groundskeeper at Forest Home when I was an intern there. A tree that is newly planted must not be overwatered. If it is, the roots will remain shallow. And when the winter snow comes, the tree will topple. When the rains come, its stability will erode away. And when the frost comes, the tree will die. No, we must only lightly water the sapling that its roots might go in search of deeper sources of water.

Deep roots are grown out of longing and need. They are driven down by discontent. They are searching for more. Depth comes from hearts that are restless. Hearts that are cautious of too easy answers. Hearts that aren't afraid of complexity. They are willing to follow the threads of their doubts. They push against the supports.

There is an uneasiness to searching. It lacks certainty. It is uncomfortable. Which is why depth, almost always, includes suffering. We would never choose it for ourselves. Instead we prefer to admire it from a distance. But suffering inevitably finds us. It comes to us, even when we are doing things well. Sometimes suffering is actually a sign that we are doing things right.

There's a song I've been listening to by one of my favorite artists, Glen Phillips. It's called "Nobody's Gonna Get Hurt" and it's about all the lies we tell ourselves. It starts with the obvious lie, "the earth is flat" (sorry if that is a spoiler for anyone) and proceeds to much more subtle fallacies, the central one being that we can somehow live life well and avoid getting our hearts broken. As I listen, I often forget the intentional delusion of the lyrics. Because some of these fallacies I still find myself latching on to . . . singing along as if they're true. Or at least telling them to my children in hopes of giving them comfort when life feels difficult.

"There's no price to love, there never was."

"We are always gonna stay young and beautiful."

"If it's meant to be, it's easy."

"Broken hearts will always mend."

"Nobody's gonna get hurt."

The underlying lie is that a pain-free life can be full and abundant. But it can't. To remain completely safe, we must live lives of control and detachment, and as a result, devoid of love. Because whole-hearted living requires vulnerability, humility, willingness to change, and therefore unavoidable heartache. Suffering.

To love others, we must engage, and when we do, we get bruised.

The German philosopher Arthur Schopenhauer presents this as the hedgehog dilemma. All of us are hedgehogs on a cold winter day. Without each other, we will freeze to death. But when we gather together, our quills poke each other. We need each other to survive and are incapable of drawing near without inflicting pain.

Without love our hearts atrophy. We cannot live without love. And heartbreak is the unavoidable consequence of love. But that doesn't mean we've done something wrong. In fact, heartbreak may just mean we're doing something right.

As I type, I am still feeling a shortness of breath. I got punched in the ribs while sparring a week ago and I haven't completely recovered from it. My daughter and I have been taking Hapkido, a Korean form of martial arts, through the city. As much as it scares me to spar, I can't wait to get back in there. Why? Because that sort of engagement makes my whole mind, body, and emotions come alive. I finish drenched in sweat and glowing, embracing my sparring partner, Tom, who is also my good friend.

But relational wounding isn't as simple as physical. My emotional defenses are much more practiced. My attacks can wound much deeper. And worst of all, my detachment, and other defenses, can leave my heart and the hearts of those I love feeling cold, lonely, and unprotected.

Reengaging usually means apologizing. Owning my mistakes. Acknowledging that I'm the one to blame. I must open myself up to the realities about myself that I'd rather avoid. But it's worth it. This is how we grow deeper. On the other side of it is freedom and connection. And this is what my heart longs for. It's what keeps us alive.

We can spend our whole lives practicing to live, theorizing about relationships, studying for a test yet to come. Or we can dive in, engage, immerse ourselves, create, and love. And yes, when we risk, we open ourselves up to getting hurt. We feel, not just joy, but pain. We get wounded and knocked down. Our hearts break. But then they mend.

And in the process we grow deeper. We experience everyday moments for the true joy that they bring. Our eyes are opened to the abundance around us. As we overcome the safety of our aloneness, as we reengage with life, we experience joy. And that joy is worth it, bruises and all.

David Whyte is a poet that I have recently come to love and appreciate. He writes this about unrequited love in his book *Consolations*:

We seem to have been born into a world where love, except for brilliant, exceptional moments, seems to exist from one side only, ours—and that may be the difficulty and the revelation and the gift—to see love as the ultimate letting go and through the doorway of that affection make the most difficult sacrifice of all, giving away the very thing we want to hold forever.

The journey toward depth is costly, because it is a progression of learning to love, and that means a constant emptying of ourselves. Happiness and comfort are not big enough to give us satisfaction and contentment, let alone meaning. Instead, we pour out our lives for the sake of others. And in this we experience life as it was meant to be lived.

C. S. Lewis writes in *The Problem of Pain*,

> The settled happiness and security which we all desire, God withholds from us by the very nature of the world: but joy, pleasure, and merriment He has scattered broadcast. . . . Our Father refreshes us on the journey with some pleasant inns, but will not encourage us to mistake them for home.

What does this mean? It means that we never arrive in this lifetime. Ever. And that is a disappointing concept to grasp. Because we long for home. We long for not just rest and refreshment, but for a sense of permanence. Not just for a brief moment of reprieve, but for never-ending stability.

And that is exactly what our lives refuse to give us. Life is in constant flux. It is filled with high points and low points. And in the midst of it all, we are constantly trying to grasp a sense of permanence. Any epiphany or moment of growth in life, our tendency is to immediately package it as a moment of enlightenment, of arrival. We've finally figured it out!

Except that this never lasts. Eventually our enlightenment turns out to be just another layer. The truth was not total truth. Instead, what is revealed is a whole new level of insecurity, doubt, and discomfort. Our certainty is replaced once again by the reminder of our transient nature. We have only just begun.

Certainty and comfort seem to go hand in hand. It brings the feeling of resolution. We are able to rest easy. With certainty comes control.

When I think of all the work I've done in spiritual direction and counseling, I have such a sense of gratitude and accomplishment. So many wounds in my heart have healed. So many shadows have been examined. So many things I've previously avoided or ignored have been brought into the open.

And yet, just the other day I was reading something, and a light went on. All of a sudden I saw common threads running through so many of the stories I tell. It revealed to me a glimpse behind the curtain—what was driving me along all the while. It revealed why I've latched on to these particular stories. These stories have allowed me to focus my attention on the deficiencies of others and conveniently avoid the pain of the jealousy I was feeling.

Maybe my friend catches a good wave and then paddles back out only to take off on another good wave while I sit out there waiting. All of a sudden my body is flooded with emotion. But rather than have to feel it, I jump immediately to how I've been wronged.

Or maybe a friend gets a promotion. It might not even be a job I'd like, but the prestige that it brings for my friend is something I deeply long for. All of a sudden I find myself judging the role, or the position, or anything honestly, that will make me feel somehow a step ahead.

Anyone I see as my equal can easily become my competition. And yet winning isn't something that inspires me or motivates me to try harder. I don't want to be the best so that I can be admired. I want to be the best, because then I don't have to feel jealous.

Jealousy . . . how I hate that feeling! It feels small and immature. It is ugly. As a type four on the enneagram, it is my nemesis. Fours long for individuality, to be special and creative and unique. And yet their individuality can create a deep insecurity that they are somehow missing a crucial piece that everyone else must possess. They long to be seen and yet not seen. And in that inner turbulence, they envy the normalcy that everyone else seems to so easily maintain.

What I'd prefer, rather than feel jealous, is to get angry. To blame another, or even life itself, for being less than it could be. It is a way of taking the moral high ground instead of staring into the eyes of the green gremlin. To have to look at my jealousy face-to-face feels like going all the way back to the starting line of my growth journey. Like drawing the cupcake in Candyland when you've almost reached the end. Like all the ground I had previously covered was for naught.

But this isn't true. While the situations, circumstances, and even the lessons themselves feel repetitive and redundant in our lives, the fact is that I have changed along the way. The issues might feel the same, but now they are deeper. I've grown. I've become deeper.

It might not feel any different in the moment. But if I take a step back, I can see that my endurance has increased. The things that were normally happening emotionally inside me are now able to be named. I have language for them, and am therefore able to separate myself a bit from their control. I have my emotions and not the other way around. I can see the thing behind the thing.

And what comes with this growth is a sort of protection. As my heart grows deeper roots, they are safer from the selfish frosts of my ego. I am able to respond early. To reengage rather than withdraw.

FOR REFLECTION AND CONVERSATION

1. When have you ever experienced a compliment that reso-nated deeply within you, as if it said, "This is who you were made to be"? Was the compliment met by any internal resis-tance in yourself?

2. How have you experienced the costliness of growth? What comforts have you had to leave behind on your journey that you would have preferred to keep?

3. What wounds or weaknesses in your heart is God revealing to you? What is God asking you to notice and name? What is the healing that God might be inviting you into?

3

ENLARGE MY HEART

We were praying for my friend Billy when Steve got a word for me. We do this from time to time at our elder board meetings. We single someone out and gather around them, lay hands on them, and pray. At first Steve thought it was a word for Billy, but, it turns out, it was for me. I'm baffled by that bit, where God corrects a wrong assumption and somehow says, "Nope, this one's for Jeff." Steve waited, quietly, until we were done praying and then asked if he could pray for me.

He said, "Jeff, God told me not to let you stay small." And that was it. Just that little bit of information. A warning? Maybe. A rebuke?

It is an interesting thing when God speaks, how it often feels so cryptic. We are waiting for God to elaborate, but he doesn't. Instead, silence. Not empty silence. More like quiet presence. I quickly wrote it down, unsure of where to go next.

These words from God come like clues. They are filled with information, even when the immediate connections are shrouded in mystery. We know we are supposed to do something, if only we knew what. Seeking and searching become a necessary part of interpretation. The information comes like a time release.

But this particular clue had me confused. Don't stay small? I could take a stab at that. I'm the pastor of a little church. In fact, we're often referred to as "the little church." Was my remaining at a little church staying small? Was I missing something? Maybe I was hiding from my true calling.

Because I do find something comforting in little. It is intimate. Everyone knows your name. No one is confused into thinking you're a bigger deal than you are. You are loved, flaws and all. To stay small feels safe.

And I know how the opposite feels as well. I came here from a big church. A great church, but honestly, one I had gotten lost in. Over my six years there, I had grown used to shaking hands with people I didn't know, but who knew me. I longed for more connected relationships.

Coming to the little church was like a drink of cool water. It satisfied a thirst I didn't know I had until I walked inside. I needed to know and be known. I was craving community. And my wife and I have found it in this sweet little church.

But now, was it time to leave? "Don't stay small." Don't hide from God's greater plan.

Don't clutch to the familiar and the safe. Be brave and step out.

I was heartbroken.

I remember praying, "God, I trust you. I'll go wherever you send me." But inside my head, my categories were in turmoil. What does it really mean to be great in God's kingdom? How am I resisting what God is doing? How am I remaining small?

But I'm learning that my initial assumptions about these words from God are usually distorted by my own biases and ways of measuring. Again and again in Scripture we're reminded that God's kingdom works on a completely different value system than ours. It is so dramatically different that it can seem upside down. Sometimes it takes paradox for us to grasp the paradigm shift. To live we must die, to lead we must serve, to win we must lose. A couple of fish and loaves are actually enough to feed the masses. The woman giving two mites is actually a much bigger deal than the man noisily drawing all the attention to his seeming generosity.

The simple, small acts of the heart reveal something much deeper and of far more value to God. He isn't distracted by outward appearances. Instead, he is after our whole heart, our surrendered will. God tells us this is the wellspring of life. From it flows that which is most precious to God: life and love.

More than a year went by, and those words from Steve, those words from God, "Don't let Jeff stay small," ended up simply as a scrawl in one of my journals somewhere. I chalked it up to mystery and moved on.

And then, one day, I was sitting with my boss, my pastor, Brad, and he was telling me that he was taking another position in a church in suburban Chicago. He was passing the leadership baton to me. He told me I was ready to fill his shoes.

Except I knew I wasn't. You see, I'm a pretty good teacher, but not a real "shepherd." I'm the introverted pastor who loves to study with the door closed. And while I'm a pretty relational guy, I only have so much to give. I needed Brad. I couldn't do this without him.

I was flooded with emotion at the thought of him leaving, overwhelmed by feelings of insecurity and inadequacy. "I can't do it," I finally blurted out. "My heart is too small."

And then I heard it, that still, small voice in the back of my head saying, "There you go, Jeff. That's what I'm talking about. I need your heart to enlarge. I need you to not stay small." I had to smile. I wasn't being asked to leave. I was being asked to grow.

I love how God's riddles take us on a journey. He leads us with such patience and care, step by step, often silent, but always there. He subtly nudges us on with just enough information for the next step or two.

And he shows us how well he knows us by addressing not only where we are going, but also pointing out where we might be resisting. Because God isn't interested in the quantity of what we have to give him, but in the percentage. He wants our whole heart. And what he cares most about is what we're clinging to in that hand behind our back. It isn't so much what we are offering, as what we're withholding.

In that clutched hand is the key to unlocking his plans for our lives, and it is also the very thing in us that wants to remain our small, false self. And mine is so connected with controlling the emotional demands on my heart. I had thought that at a small church, as an assistant pastor, I would be better able to manage those demands. I could keep it under control.

But when I do this, I inevitably set the bar way too low. I become possessive of my time. I operate out of my need for comfort. I avoid risk and pain. I hesitate to enter into another's pain.

There can be a convenient misperception of humility in staying small. It has been a good defensive strategy for me. You can't be accused of trying too hard, or trying and failing, or failing at all. Small looks modest. It can wonderfully mask our deep insecurities. It is an easy place to hide.

I make excuses for staying small. It isn't my personality or gift mix. If God wanted me to do it, he'd have made me better at it, right? But this too is a distortion.

When God speaks our whole world usually gets upended. It has to if we are to grow. Things must get flipped right side up. He changes our perceptions, so that we're finally seeing how we were meant to see. He shows us where we are resisting. He points out where we're holding back. How we have become comfortable and satisfied. And he gently loosens our clutching fingers until we trust him enough to let it go.

Psalm 119:32 tells us, "I will run in the way of your commandments when you enlarge my heart!" (ESV). And that is just what he has been doing to mine. Stretching and pulling, often in ways that have felt unbearable. But as my heart has grown, so has my ability to give and receive love. To know and to be known.

A friend of mine once warned me that "God will insist on your greatness." I don't know about you, but that statement makes me incredibly uncomfortable. But if you substitute the word *greatness* with *glory*, you find that it is very biblical. I like how C. S. Lewis, in his sermon "The Weight of Glory," talks about our desires and pleasures being too small. He says, "If we consider the unblushing promises of reward and the staggering nature of the rewards promised in the Gospels, it would seem that Our Lord finds our desires, not too strong, but too weak."

This idea of glory might feel a bit abstract. Dallas Willard, from the glossary on his website, defines it like this: "Glory is the magnificent outpouring of the radiant splendor of God's power, strength, beauty, and goodness." I don't know about you, but I could certainly use more of that in my life!

It isn't wrong to want glory. But God withholds it not because it is wrong, but because it is dangerous. Our hearts must be made ready. And the path toward readiness is the way of humility. But humility is never the end in itself. Humility is preparation for glory. The two are intimately connected. Without humility, glory consumes us. It creates an insatiable appetite that gnaws at our soul. But with humility, we become properly self-forgetful, and we can shine without becoming consumed by our own self-love.

When I next met with my spiritual director, I told her about the recent revelation. I told her that the word I had heard so long ago, to not stay small, was all of a sudden answered. It was my heart all along. And she simply smiled and said, "Brilliant!" She's right. He is. When God speaks, we realize just how intimately he knows us, as we are and as we will someday be. And he knows just what to say and exactly how and when to say it.

It was in the middle of a friend's sermon when God gave me another nudge. We share the pulpit at my church and that morning I wasn't preaching. I was able to just sit back and take notes. The sermon was insightful, deep, intelligent . . . all the things I secretly aspire to. All of sudden I felt like I was listening to myself. I could picture myself up there preaching, offering a smart and semi-obscure reference that creates just the right amount of impressiveness without sounding pedantic. Here was someone with a gift similar to mine. A teacher. I could see the similarity in what we offered and therefore in what I perceived as our value to the church community.

God whispered quietly, "This isn't what I need from you." It wasn't a statement of correction or criticism. It was as if God was saying, "Jeff, this isn't where your value lies."

Which was followed by that flash of resistance, or inner protest. "But I'm a teacher."

God pushed back, "You're a pastor."

My resistance became defensiveness.

"No I'm not."

I do know that's my title—pastor—but, again, that is not my strength. And while I am adequate relationally, I lack the emotional stamina. I often have felt like God gave me a good engine, but it came with an embarrassingly small fuel tank. I can run fast and efficiently, just not for very long. It is humiliating to me. I feel, socially, like Cinderella, knowing that when the clock strikes midnight, the carriage turns back into a pumpkin, and I start saying all the wrong things.

And honestly, beneath the embarrassment and insecurity is resentment. My introversion sometimes feels as if it's a handicap, a disability. I compensate by strengthening other areas in my life. If I can't be the relational guy, at least I can be the smart one. I love reading, thinking, contemplating. How can I leverage those gifts in such a way that I can maintain my value? And though this is exhausting and stressful, it at least offers the possibility of feeling stronger.

But God was pushing me out of this pattern. It was as if he was correcting my misshapen identity. Because my false self wants to be seen in the best, most positive light. And that necessarily implies my talents and abilities, right? My weaknesses can go back into the shadows where they belong.

But that word from God felt like I was being named according to what I knew was lacking. The nudge was toward weakness. That this is where the power lies.

As the sermon ended, I went about my in-between service duties of greeting, praying, and otherwise engaging with this church that I love so much. As the second service began, and I took a seat next to my friend before he spoke again, I got another nudge. We were being led in prayer in preparation for the sermon, and God told me to put my hand on my friend's shoulder. Now, this is a small gesture, but not a natural one for me and this particular friend. There was a risk involved. It was a bit more intimate for him and me. I have plenty of friends with whom I wouldn't have given it a second thought, but with this guy it was different. But my response was simply to obey.

As I reached out my hand I felt a crazy jolt of emotion, like a rush of electricity. I'm serious. I'm surprised my hair didn't stand on end. It was like a surge of love. It wasn't my love. It was way, way bigger. I felt like a conduit. I felt God's love for this man. It was overwhelming. It was humbling. I had never felt that much love. Not ever.

I felt myself asking God the question, "Do you love me that much?" It was almost incomprehensible. My limited supply of love was simply a drop in the ocean of his. I had this all wrong! I had been rationing out spoonfuls of love when there was a firehose of it just that close.

What a huge shift in paradigm. It reminds me now of Paul saying in 1 Corinthians that he delights in his weaknesses. For when he is

weak, then he is strong. I've been able to quote that verse since very
early Sunday school days, but have never taken it so literally. Humility is nice, but no one wants a weak leader.

But this isn't true. Because the largest, most generous heart of
man has infinitely less to offer than God's heart. So God chooses the
weak things to confound the wise. He can display his glory through
them without distortion. It allows for the divine to slip through the
cracks in the natural world and be seen in all its fullness of power
and glory.

There is a parable from Jesus where he talks about how we invest
what God has given us. In the story, the servants with the greater
amounts invest and receive double on their return. The servant with
one talent hides it. The one with the least amount refuses to invest
out of fear. Instead, he hides. He remains small.

We were discussing this story in church and afterward a friend
commented on how tempted we are to hide our one-talent gifts.
That might not quite be the point of the story, but it is worth thinking
about. The one with the least to give incorrectly assumed God was
stingy. And that his one talent was inconsequential. He had no
vision for how it might be used.

But what if God asks us to give an account for the gifts we feel
are our weakest? What if we are accountable for how we invest our
weaknesses? What if my limited emotional energy wasn't a weakness,
but an opportunity? Maybe instead of loving people out of the abundance of my heart, I could instead offer them something of far
greater value. God's enormous heart flowing through my small heart.

And maybe enlarging our hearts is not increasing our natural
abilities, but instead is the increase in courage to lean into our
weaknesses—to allow them to come out into the light, and to see
God multiply our humble offerings.

Hudson Taylor, the great missionary to China, said, "God's work, done in God's way, will not lack God's supply." But God's way is the way of humility. It is the way of meekness. It is painfully honest about its limitations, and yet opens the door for provision far beyond what we can ask or imagine.

As wonderful as it was to feel that love of God for my friend, part of me wanted so badly to withdraw my hand. I felt God telling me to keep it there. So I did. Afterward my friend came up and told me that he too had felt something powerful in that moment. He told me that he felt like God was praying for him.

It requires discipline and obedience to serve in weakness. It is unnatural. It requires discipline and obedience to lay aside one's eloquence and giftedness, and instead simply bring the possibility of God's presence. But there is no comparison between the two. My simple offering of loaves and fish is nothing compared to God's banquet, and yet both matter. The simple gesture of obedience and the courage to remain in that place of humbling transparency creates the opportunity.

FOR REFLECTION AND CONVERSATION

1. Where do you prefer to stay small and safe? Are there invitations from God that you resist or hide from?

2. Is there a clutching hand behind your back? What does it contain? What are you afraid will happen if you let it go?

3. How is God insisting on your glory? That is, where does God want you to enlarge?

4. What is the courageous next step God may be calling you to?

DISCOVERING OUR TRUE VOCATION

I HAVE ALWAYS BEEN A BIT OF A WALLFLOWER. To this day, I often take the posture of a detached observer, cautiously waiting for an opportunity to safely engage. Wondering where I fit in or if I belong. Secretly hoping that I'll be noticed, but too terrified to actually test the waters. Deep down, longing for the courage to join in the dance, and simultaneously terrified at the prospect. If only someone would just pull me in.

One of the best days of my life happened when I was in seventh grade. I'm thirteen and less than a year into a new school and a new town. I'm still the "new guy," no longer eating lunch by myself, but a long way from having any real friends. We're nearing the end of the school year and much to my chagrin, there is a dance scheduled to take place during regular school hours. I'm terrified. There's no way out of this, and I hate dancing.

I shuffle into the darkened gym, the latest Thompson Twins song playing loudly in the background.

Oh, oh, hold me now (hold me in your lovin' arms),
Oh warm my heart (warm my cold and tired heart) . . .

I scan the room for an empty span of wall to lean against (and try to disappear). That's my plan. I'll park myself for the next hour until I can finally escape from the suffocating anxiety of loneliness. I just want out of here.

And then it happens. Straight out of a John Hughes movie, Becky—the best-looking girl at the school, in my opinion—walks up to me. She doesn't even ask me to dance. She just grabs my hand and pulls me out onto the dance floor as Cyndi Lauper begins to sing, *Lyin' in my bed, I hear the clock tick, and think of you . . .*

It's her ballad "Time After Time." A *slow* song.

With no time to panic, even though I don't have a clue what I'm doing, I just go with it. At the end of the song, Becky thanks me and I stammer a barely audible "thanks" in return. But honestly, I can't believe I didn't pass out.

Afterward, some of my new friends chided me, but I couldn't have cared less. That dance was pure bliss. I still get all warm and fuzzy when I hear that song today. *Suitcase of memories, time after . . .*

That moment was transcendent. What I mean is that those four minutes on the dance floor carried me beyond my inhibitions and into my true heart's desire. Beyond the comfortability and safety of the gym wall and out into the place of both fear and longing.

But, as triumphant as that day remains in my mind, thirty years later, my default setting is still *wallflower*.

Whenever there's dancing at a wedding reception I fret. My wife is a terrific dancer—it's in her heart and soul. I love that about her. And I know how disappointed she'll be if we don't dance. That adds its own pressure. She's gotten used to my protests and has realized that it always is worth asking me again, or better yet, just grabbing my hand and pulling me onto the dance floor. Even if I shake my head no, inside I'm hoping she'll persist. Because, in the end, that is where I long to be. Dancing together brings us so much intimacy.

And intimacy doesn't come easy. While it may always be the fantasy—that somehow intimacy is stumbled upon, or simply comes naturally—it doesn't. Not the real stuff. True intimacy is found by pressing through the anxiety, by disarming self-protection, by taking risks. Intimacy exposes us, brings us to a place of real transparency, and moves us beyond the head and into the heart.

In the play *The Great God Brown* there is a line that illustrates perfectly what I'm getting at: "Why am I afraid to dance, I who love music and rhythm and grace and song and laughter? Why am I afraid to live, I who love life and the beauty of flesh and the living colors of the earth and sky and sea? Why am I afraid to love, I who love love?"

I think the answer is that we fall in love with the idea of love. It is so much safer to live in the world of our thoughts and opinions and to remain aloof, disengaged from our heart's deepest longings. But it is a restless comfort. Our hearts refuse to be still.

So God, in his brilliance, guides us into that place of vulnerability, and ultimately, freedom. He pushes us into our calling and attacks the pride that holds us back. It is a noticeable pattern that shows itself in almost every story told in Scripture. God presents a vision and then asks for it back. God promises freedom and then leads his people into the wilderness. In all of this, God prepares the hearts of his people for a vision greater than they can comprehend.

When God speaks, it creates a tension. But what is God after, ultimately? Is my true identity one of glory or humility? Lifting of the heart and dying of the ego can feel mutually opposed, almost contradictory.

God is asking us to be both great and small. Somehow, the answer is both of these at once. And there is a tension created as God pulls us in both directions. It is in this tension that our hearts become free.

Because we are made for glory. God insists on it. And yet glory is so often the thing that destroys the soul. It corrupts us and leaves us craving the very things that poison true glory. Our longing for self-glorification corrodes it. The very thing God desires for us to have, he cannot, in clear conscience, bestow on us without doing more harm than good.

Like a craving for nicotine, we long to be adored. That broken part of us craves to be regarded as magnificent. We insist on being recognized for our accomplishments. Only in the state of humility is our heart protected from our selfish ego. But even our humility is vulnerable.

I love that scene from the television show *The Office*, where Michael Scott says that if he were rich he would give money anonymously to build a hospital wing and then, when asked, he would quietly confess to knowing who built it. "It was Michael Scott," he would say.

"But how do you know that?"

"Because I'm him."

Like most of the humor in *The Office*, the awkward truth cuts deep. None of us would actually speak such a thought out loud. Only Michael Scott is oblivious enough to admit to it. But we'd think it.

How do we live into the glorious future God has for us without allowing our vanity and insecurity to consume us in the process?

When I try to control this dilemma on my own, I usually end up diminishing myself. I disengage. I decide not to compete. I sit in the back or stand against the wall. I refuse to engage. I avoid the vanity of success by refusing to participate.

But God has this way of insisting on our greatness. God pulls us away from the wall, out of the shadows and onto the dance floor. He asks us to lean in, to advance, to engage.

There's an ancient spiritual discipline known as the *examen*. The basic idea is that, at the end of the day, you reflect back and ask yourself where you felt closest to God and where you felt the farthest. Often the words used are consolation and desolation. They indicate the direction we are moving, toward or away from God's active presence in the world. The texture of consolation is more than mere

happiness. It is growing in love and faith and mercy. Desolation, op-
positely, feels like disconnection, loneliness, anxiety, and doubt.

Our lives oscillate between these poles and God has a way of
using both for our good. He is with us in the green pastures and also
in the valley of shadow.

I've noticed this pattern in my own life. There are sometimes
whole seasons of either consolation or desolation. The frequency
varies considerably. And sometimes they both arrive concurrently.

One day started with the pleasant surprise of opening up my
laptop and seeing six or seven congratulatory emails waiting in my
inbox. It took me a minute to figure out what they even were talking
about. Subject lines such as, "Way to go!" or "Just read the article"
caught me a bit off guard. What article?

As I read further, I finally pieced together the fact that a dear
friend of mine, an accomplished author, had quoted my doctoral
dissertation in an article she'd published in a national magazine. My
first time in print. Some classmates and friends had stumbled across
it and knew that even something as simple as being quoted was a
pretty big deal for me.

I clicked on the article and read it through. Actually I first scanned
for my name and read the quote. I didn't even remember writing it,
but it sounded good. I then backed up to the beginning and read the
whole thing start to finish. As I did, my email alerts kept dinging
with more and more affirmation. It was turning out to be a great day.

And then one more ding. I glanced down at my inbox and saw
an email response to a job application I had submitted a few weeks
earlier. The position advertised sounded perfect for me: a pastor
in residence (at the seminary from which I had graduated) with
experience in the areas of philosophy of mind and metaphysics.
Bingo! I am embarrassed now to admit that I thought I was shoe
in. How many pastors do you know who have studied human
consciousness? Right.

But there it was: a rejection.

"Thank you so much for applying. Maybe next time." Something to that effect. I was devastated. Humiliated. I wanted to crawl under my desk and hide. *I should have known. Of course they don't want me. What do I have to offer, anyway?*

Now, I've been through ups and downs, but that had to be a personal record for plumbing the slough of despair. Back-to-back glory and rejection. And on my day off, of all days. My mind and emotions swung and dipped, slowly rising only to plummet again like a roller coaster. Utterly whipsawed.

I grabbed my journal and a pen and took off out the door. Three things usually help in moments such as these: walking, writing, and more coffee. (Or surfing, but the waves that day were flat.) I walked down the hill by my house, into the town shopping district a few blocks away, and grabbed a table at one of our local coffee shops. I ordered, sat down, and began scribbling my thoughts.

Why is success so difficult that I can't keep myself from turning it into some narcissistic fantasy? Why is true glory so fleeting? Why can't I receive it without twisting it into something so self-aggrandizing?

And why did this rejection hurt so badly? What was I looking for from my seminary? Is there some sort of authoritative validation I'm missing? After all these years, why am I not more secure?

And God, what is next for me? Am I doing enough with what I've been given? Should I be trying harder? Should I be more content with what I have? What am I supposed to be when I grow up?

As my thoughts came faster, my writing grew more hurried and less legible. Finally, I realized that someone had approached my table and was standing there silently, politely waiting for an opportunity to interrupt.

"Excuse me, but are you the pastor at that little white church up the hill?" a man's voice said.

I looked up and saw an unfamiliar face with round glasses, a bit older than myself, with a big smile and an Indiana Jones-style hat on his head.

"Yeah, I am," I said.

"I'm not a Christian," he blurted, "but I've been to your church a few times."

I nodded and smiled at the confession. "How'd you like it?" I asked.

"Well, I just wanted to tell you that when you speak, I find it really, well, moving. I was wondering if you'd be willing to get coffee with me sometime and talk about some faith questions I have," he said.

"Of course I would."

We exchanged numbers and emails, shook hands and said goodbye. As he turned and walked away, I heard God say something:

"Just do that, Jeff."

And with that came such peace. All the worry about who I am or how I am perceived melted away in that moment. For a brief second, I was a little boy sitting at the feet of his father, hearing the words his heart longed for: "Well done." I felt free.

It was as if God were saying, "Just be yourself, Jeff. Let me handle the rest."

The fact is, God is really good at handling the rest. The hard part, the place where God respectfully restrains himself, is in matters of our heart and will. God refuses to choose for us. God offers opportunity. As Lewis says in *The Screwtape Letters*, "He cannot ravish. He can only woo."

If I could pick my future, if I had my way, I'd have everyone sitting at my feet as I shared insight after insight with them. This is where I feel valuable. This is what I would describe as consolation. I feel strong and powerful. Just as long as I don't say anything I regret.

I remember one time my spiritual director asked me if I always felt the pressure to say something insightful. I lowered my head a bit and sheepishly admitted yes. I'll never forget her response. Without any judgment she simply said, "That sounds exhausting."

Without hesitation I blurted out, "It is!"

We are so bad at choosing what is best for us. If my identity is found in saying the right thing at the right time, I've created an unsustainable system of validation. I am always one foolish statement away from feeling horrible about myself. And deep down, if I'm honest, I know I'm a fraud.

Because I'm not that insightful. I just read a lot. I can quote impressive people and glide along on their intellectual coattails. It works to some extent. I just find myself personally unconvinced.

Now the man standing at the table at the coffee shop that one day has, since, become a dear friend. His name is Paul. We get together and he asks me question after question about my faith, about Christianity, about Jesus. I do my best, but often I have to admit that his questions are my own. I point back to what I've seen God do in my own heart and life. More than anything, I just try to be as honest as possible.

Recently he thanked me for this. He told me what he appreciated most about our lunches together was my transparency. I admitted that he probably knows more about my faith, what I really, deep down believe, than just about anyone else in my life. I realized that Paul is more than someone to minister to. God has used him to feed my soul. He has given me the sacred space where I can simply be me.

Now this doesn't mean that I'm being dishonest with my church. I don't push anything I don't firmly believe in. But I am careful. I know what a mess words can make, and how their effect on people can create deep misunderstanding that can undermine trust. If my church doesn't trust me, I can't lead.

But what Paul has taught me is that the most trustworthy thing I can do is to admit those things I don't know or understand. At least to him. To someone. I think this is why when God said to me, "Just do that," he meant just be yourself. Not impressive, but instead transparent. Not insightful, but honest. Part of me doesn't even know where to begin. And the other part has never wanted anything more than that.

I'm realizing that this is all God has ever wanted from me. To lay aside the expectations of others, and to be who he has made me to be. That is all he wants from any of us, from each one of us.

What we find in the intersection of glory and humility is intimacy and freedom. It is filled with joy. These moments are often quick and fleeting, but they occur. As the pendulum of our hearts swings back and forth between these poles, there are moments when our true selves emerge. There is a texture to these moments of vulnerability, and simultaneously, a detached confidence. It is almost self-forgetful. We are captivated.

I've recently started taking dance lessons with my wife. I bought them for her for her birthday. I knew she'd be delighted. I also knew the actual cost wasn't the money I was spending. It was my self-esteem. I hate that feeling of being inexperienced and inadequate. Who wants to be that guy?

And, as you can guess, it has been wonderful. Sometimes I'm trying so hard not to mess up that I forget I have a dance partner. But as I learn the steps, I'm starting to lead, to frame, to be strong. And I watch Patty light up. Man, there's nothing better. It is so intimate.

No wonder the word that was given to describe the heart of the triune God was *perichoresis*, from which we get the word choreography. The love of God is this beautiful picture of joyous movement. This intimate dance is what we're invited into. It requires us to stand up straight, to yield, to let go, and to savor the goodness of the moment. To feel the joy of dancing.

This was Jesus' prayer. That we would be drawn into this dance with God. John 17:23 says, "I in them and you in me—so that they may be brought to complete unity. Then the world will know that you sent me and have loved them even as you have loved me."

And this is the secret to transformation. To remain in the tension is to give yourself to the dance. To yield to the flow. To get swept up by the river. In the midst of that flow come times of both consolation and desolation. Times of glory and times of humility. It is intimate, vulnerable, thrilling, and nerve racking.

To stay in the flow requires us to let go of what feels secure, that illusion of control, and to trust, to submit. Because this is the place of delight, not in the highs or the lows, but in the intimacy and vulnerability of being ourselves and forgetting ourselves.

That is the invitation.

FOR REFLECTION AND CONVERSATION

1. Maybe you aren't afraid to dance, but certainly there is some area in your life that you avoid at all costs. What is it that feels so risky? What is it about whatever your "dancing" might be that makes you feel vulnerable and exposed?

2. Do you relate to the tension between glory and humility? Where do you most feel moments of consolation? What causes you to feel desolate?

3. Is there a way for you to press into your fear and take a step towards vulnerability? What would the risk be? What might be the glory on the other side?

PART 2

NECESSARY SEASONS

MENTIONED EARLIER THAT THE STRAIGHT LINE I drew toward transformation is misleading. Life isn't straight.

Our stories wander through seasons of vision, followed by times of desert and brokenness. We find ourselves being renewed, and at other times, feeling abandoned. At times we are filled with life, and other times deep despair. And God is, somehow, in both.

There is a pattern to this as well. It isn't new. It is the paschal mystery that has been seen and experienced for hundreds of years. It is the way of Jesus, and is illustrated by his birth, death, and resurrection. This mystery fills every page of Scripture, of nature, and our own lives. We see it in the circularity of our seasons, from summer, to fall, to winter, and back to spring.

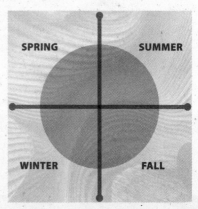

But over time, I think it is best illustrated as a wave.

I'll say more about this as we go. But this pattern is not just another illustration. Instead, it fits within the first structure.

So instead of a nice straight line, we get a wavy one, a path that bends and twists.

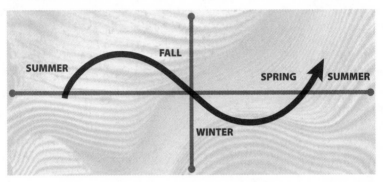

This is so important to remember when circumstances in life take a downward turn. When we are blindsided by disappointment and loss. When our visions die or our optimism fades. When the warmth we once felt is replaced by cold and dreary days. We remember that these winter seasons are both vital for our growth and graciously transitory. They do unique work. And they too will pass.

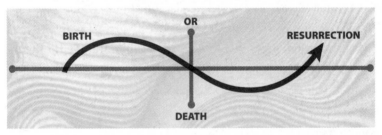

5

THE IMPORTANCE
OF DESOLATION

I LOVE THE IDEA OF GROWTH and transformation. It is a wonderful invitation to freedom. It is an offering of deeper joy. The only problem is that it costs so much. It isn't just pain, but often suffering. The small self within us is withering. And it can go on and on.

Sometimes it isn't even our own growth that is costing us so much. Sometimes it is the growth in others that is causing the disruption. And to us, things are just fine as they were. The change is unwelcome. The disruption feels unwanted, unnecessary, and threatening.

And if we aren't careful, another's growth can throw us into despair.

I remember a time when I lived in that place of despair for several really dark days. It happened because my wife, Patty, is growing. She's blossoming, thriving, stretching, and it's bringing her to life. With her growth come opportunities. It is exciting to watch. But it also triggers some deeper worries and fears in me.

The parts of her that recently have been coming to life aren't the ones that I readily encourage. Those areas of growth have been happening all along our eighteen-year journey. My spiritual growth, my natural interests, what I read, what I learn, all come out in our everyday conversations. We spur each other on in this way and do so with relative ease. I have always enjoyed the depth of connection we experience.

But this new growth is more in her extraversion, her athleticism, her passion for coaching and drive for success. These are things I respect about her and am attracted to, but aren't necessarily strengths of my own. Some can even be weaknesses, or worse, insecurities. As she grows in these new ways, I can tend to shrink back. I feel judged, or inferior, or inadequate. I start to feel threatened or scared. Like maybe I'm not enough for her.

Because of her recent successes, she was awarded a free trip to the annual meeting for her new business. It is a week-long experience, filled with like-minded coaches and fitness professionals. She can't wait. And I, maybe for the first time, am feeling left behind, worried that the life I've provided won't live up to the life she's being presented with. That I'll either be abandoned, or settled for.

These feelings aren't based on any real truths or experiences. Maybe that one time my girlfriend dumped me for one of my best friends when I was a sophomore in high school, but that feels so ridiculous to say out loud. Maybe it comes from so many movies that use marital unfaithfulness as an inevitable plotline. All of a sudden my life is becoming fatal attraction or an affair to remember. But even worse, the feeling like I'm not the main character of the movie anymore. Instead, I'm the jealous spouse. The pitiable supporting actor.

I am embarrassed to admit it, but I think the feeling of being sidelined or secondary is often the deeper offense. My ego longs to be front and center. To be the one adored. I can't tolerate it if that were to be another thing, person, vision, career. How dare Patty adore something besides me! How dare this new love intrude and cause such confusion.

And this is the range of my despair. Within this space, adoration is mine by right, and the lack of it, or even the potential lack of it, feels like betrayal. I've been victimized. And so I retreat safely back into this sphere and console myself. Yes, life may fall apart. I may be left behind. But if I detach first, it will hurt less. And then I will rebuild a life that is immune from ever being hurt like this again. I will create a safe, detached new life that is invulnerable.

How do I remain present when my emotional fears are wreaking havoc on my self-confidence?

The increase of responsibilities in life can feel like adding weight to a backpack. With a manageable load, you don't even really need a waist belt. But when that load exceeds a certain amount, or when the distance you must travel exceeds a certain number of miles, you'd better make sure you're wearing your pack right.

As someone who loves backpacking, I've learned that there are certain rules to fitting your pack right. A novice assumes one carries the weight with the shoulders. And you can, but not well, and not for long. That works only for loads that are well within our comforts. But if we're serious about carrying some true weight, something approaching our actual abilities, we have to put that weight where it belongs. On our hips. Our shoulders then are only steadying the load. Our skeletal structure starts doing the work, and not just our muscles. With proper alignment, we find we can carry much more than we initially thought possible.

I love that verse where Jesus talks about his yoke or burden for our lives. Each of us has one. And the good news is, that according to him, it is light and easy. Even though it often doesn't feel that way. Sometimes it feels enormously heavy. Sometimes I think I'm going to fall over, collapse, or, worse yet, turn back.

At this point of despair, I'm often tempted to protest against God's discernment of my abilities. "Why are you asking me to bear this too? My pack feels full, heavy enough, maybe even too heavy. There isn't room for this added burden and certainly I cannot be expected to carry more!"

But it is in moments like this that I'm slowly realizing that I am the one that is mishandling the burden. That my metaphorical waist belt has come unfastened. I'm carrying the load entirely with my shoulders and they are slumping under the weight. I must readjust the load, not set it down. And sometimes this readjustment feels counterintuitive. I want to use my spiritual muscles and strength, when, in fact, it is all about alignment. I need to do less work and instead, carry it in the right way.

If I take it on faith that the weight I'm carrying is the right amount, then I can simply focus on where the problem actually lies—in my own stubborn desire to carry things the way I choose, or in those too familiar patterns of how I used to behave.

This is so difficult for me, because it often conflicts and intrudes into the privacy of my love for my own desolate despair. These realms are usually at odds. My desolation is my place of safety and comfort, where I withdraw and tell myself I am safe from the constant evaluation of others. In this quiet dark room, I am enough. At least that is what I tell myself. It is a place of lonely detachment, but at least it feels safe.

Faith is the opposite of detachment. It's being invited out of the cave where I've withdrawn and stepping into the light of truth and reality. It offers hope, but also comes at such a cost.

David Whyte, in *Consolations*, writes,

> Despair is a haven with its own temporary form of beauty; of self-compassion, it is the invitation we accept when we want to remove ourselves from hurt. Despair is a last protection. To disappear through despair, is to seek a temporary but necessary illusion, a place where we hope nothing can ever find us in the same way again.

The danger is not the despair. The danger is that we can prefer its darkness to the light of truth. Despair doesn't ask us to change or grow. It lets us remain small. It gives us permission to avoid life's challenges. It allows us to pretend to be sick and skip school instead of bucking up and taking the test we don't feel ready for.

Growing up, I loved getting sick. It gave, and still gives, me permission to withdraw. To crawl in bed. To sleep, to rest, to read, to binge-watch Netflix. And we do need days like this. Occasionally. But, if we're not careful, this can become our vision of the good life. Comfort can become the goal. And a comfortable life, a risk-free life, is a life of detachment, avoidance, and checking out. And our bodies can learn to do this without us even being conscious of the fact. When life gets threatening, we retreat to our island.

And when we do, we create a wake of turmoil. And I'm not even talking about all the tasks we leave undone, or the phone calls that are left unanswered, or the assignments that pile up. The greater offense, at least for me, has been to my family and companions on my journey. To move away from life's vulnerabilities is to cut ourselves off relationally. My despair becomes theirs. My avoidance communicates my own self-obsession. My detachment wounds my dearest relationships.

Nothing is ever really solved in this space. Instead my mind just races to worst-case scenarios and hopeless feelings of inevitability. I feel doomed. How did I not see it before? I start preparing for the worst.

When it's your marriage, these thoughts are toxic, even fatal. The one person you need becomes your greatest threat. There can be no compromise. Any movement feels threatening. Because when one spouse grows, so must the other. Either both of you grow, or both of you stay small. Either our love is generative, or it is degenerative.

And in my case, growing almost always involves increased generosity. It asks for more of my precious time. More of my heart. To surrender my ego. To love Patty like I love myself.

This is all well and good when I feel like I'm getting something out of the deal, when my love for her is clearly reciprocated by her love for me. But what if it just costs me? What if her growth leaves me in this place of inadequacy? What if my generosity abandons me in the defenseless posture of vulnerability, inadequately defended? Alone in my weakness. What if I lose?

Everything in me rebels. My skin crawls. Bitterness and resentment start flowing through my veins. The worries and fears become visceral pains. My shoulders ache and stoop. My head throbs.

But this is right where the battle begins. This is the place where courage shines. This is where victory is fought and won.

In desolation, we have the opportunity for increased self-awareness. To peer into the deep waters of the heart and to see the crocodiles swimming around in there. Our selfishness cannot hide. Our pettiness is exposed. We are confronted with our own anger, self-loathing, and shame. And to see and name these things can cause them to shrivel and wither in the light of truth. But it takes courage to draw them out.

Often the light reveals that everything is, actually, okay. Of course, not always. But often my gloom is caught up in all the potential fears, and not reality. I see where things could lead, and pretty soon, the possibility is replaced by inevitability. I start to experience the pain as if the rejection has already occurred. Reality is so distorted by the fantasy that when it is exposed to the light of truth, it is almost like awakening from a dream. The smoke starts to clear. The picture comes slowly into focus.

But a part of me still rebels. Because, in the real world, I am no longer the victim. I no longer hold the moral high ground. I am exchanging truth for the distorted pleasure of being right. And part of me would much prefer being right. Even when it causes division, when it creates detachment, and when it pushes me back into a posture of lonely defensiveness. At least in despair I feel right. And for my ego, for my small, false self, that is everything. That is my drug of choice.

To choose truth is to choose life. It is to grow and breathe. To become more alive. To become more myself. To be transformed. To be redeemed.

But it is also choosing death. Death to my ego. Depriving that small voice of its place of authority. Maybe even kicking it to the curb. Like a bully that has always sort of protected us, but has held us back and kept us small. It's time for him to go. And interestingly enough, when we finally get the nerve to shove him out of the room, we don't miss him. It has cost us nothing.

As my jealousy and insecurity came forward into the light, what became so painfully clear is that my feelings of distrust weren't about Patty at all. Behind it lurked distrust, not for my wife but for God. Distrust that these feelings of suffering were somehow connected to a mistake that God had made and not there out of God's design. Because that would mean that I wasn't just wrong about my feelings and withdrawal. It would mean that I was avoiding the very thing I needed. That somehow, on the other side of this humiliation lay healing and restoration and freedom. That somehow, this desolation wasn't just allowed by God. It was an invitation.

To love another at one's own expense requires a level of confidence I wasn't sure I possessed. But all of a sudden I knew one thing for sure. That is who I wanted to be. To possess the self-confidence to love with courage. To love without fear and timidity.

I raced into the room where Patty was sitting with feet propped up on our big leather chair. "I have something I want to say to you," I blurted out. She looked at me quizzically, not quite sure what to prepare herself for. More accusations? I paused, feeling the weight of the words I was about to say becoming magnified as they neared verbalization. "I trust you." I said it as a fact. As if I was just discovering it myself for the first time. It wasn't that I was choosing to trust her, although I suppose that was included. I simply did. I do. And saying that to Patty sent waves of gratitude crashing over me.

I'm always amazed at how much power there is in simply naming something. Until we do, these conflicting ideas or beliefs are free to cohabit our internal spaces. These two voices of trust and suspicion are competing for the same chair at the table, and to verbalize one of them, to recognize the emotion out loud, is like giving it the chair. The opposing voice shuffles around a bit, but finally leaves.

To tell Patty that I trusted her offered that seat at the table to not only trust, but with it intimacy and vulnerability. As suspicion left, so did my self-protection and fear. At least for the moment. It was like the foggy haze began to burn off and the sun began to break through.

I trusted Patty, and even more significantly, I trusted God. I trusted him that Patty is exactly what I need in my life at this point in time. Which means that God is using her strength and growth to directly press on my areas of discomfort, and even my painful insecurity. That the emotions being revealed, the deep fears being unearthed, the paranoia and inferiority, are being intentionally disturbed. This isn't some sort of design flaw or sign of incompatibility. Instead, it is another depiction of God's brilliance and even kindness. God is taking my marriage, once a place of deep stability, and using it for the purpose of creating instability. Because this is how transformation begins.

FOR REFLECTION AND CONVERSATION

1. Have you ever felt discouraged by another's growth? What was the insecurity that prevented you from celebrating with them?

2. How do you protect yourself when you feel threatened? What is really at risk?

3. The victory in desolation is when we give up the safety of being the victim and embrace the opportunity for increased self-awareness and growth. I find that the courage comes when I trust the longing and move forward with the confidence that I'm being led. How does this match your experience with desolation? How might God's presence provide enough safety to risk it?

6

THE ILLUMINATION OF WAITING

PATTY IS ORIGINALLY FROM SEATTLE. Seattle is still home for her, and so every summer we make a pilgrimage to the Pacific Northwest to visit friends and family. And every year I am reminded of the fact that there is nowhere as beautiful as Washington in July or August. It is gorgeous and warm. Bright blue skies matched by green everywhere. You can't beat Seattle in the summer.

But sometimes we make the journey in December for Christmas. And during the winter, it is an entirely different world. Each day gray and dreary. Not necessarily rainy. More like a constant drizzling wetness, and it can last for days on end.

Often the winter seasons of life are like this. Day after day of gray skies and drippy weather. We long for a bit of sunshine, but it never seems to come. And so we wait, and wait. We remain indoors, often becoming more and more lethargic.

So much of life involves waiting. And it can seem to go on indefinitely. It's like someone has pressed the pause button, but we have no idea for how long. It's like staring at the progress bar of a software update that is frozen and we start to wonder if maybe the system has crashed. My impulse in these moments is often to start banging the spacebar on the keyboard . . . as if that has ever helped anything, ever.

We all can be so impatient. Which is one of the reasons, I believe, that God makes us wait. In fact, it is the most loving thing God can do. To offer us the opportunity to detox from our hurried expectations. To practice remaining still and unhurried. But if I'm honest, I hate it.

I'm waiting for something right now. And it's driving me crazy. All I want is an indication that things are moving. But so far, nothing. All my feeler emails have gone unanswered. And so I search for the meaning in the uncomfortable silence. Is this bad news? Maybe they are just preoccupied. Should I send another email? Will I appear too desperate?

The opportunity I'm waiting on first came with what felt like an annunciation. Not an angel or a divine proclamation, but enough clarity and coincidence in the timing that it made me perk up. I had mentioned something to my wife about a desire of my heart, only to have a friend respond, completely separately, with a text, about the very possibility I had stated to Patty. And then I was at dinner the next night and a couple of friends I ran into brought it up out of the blue and had a connection that might help. In just a short couple of days a dream had transformed into a very real possibility. And I had done nothing but sit back and watch. Once again I marveled at God's brilliance, his efficiency, and how little he needs my efforts to bring something about.

Except that it has been two weeks since all of that and it has been radio silence ever since. Nothing. I even sent out the allowable follow-up emails, testing the waters. Again, silence. I find myself journaling "What is this all about?!"

Because, if it was up to me, I'd have just left matters as they were. Why stir my heart only to disappoint it? Why mess with my self-protective boundaries that are careful to dream only simple, attainable dreams? Why raise the expectations to a point where they can be disappointed?

But the fact is, I have no reason to be disappointed. Not yet. I haven't received bad news. I simply have no news. But it actually isn't the painful letdown that I'm afraid of. No, the pain *is* the waiting. It's in the angst that boils to the surface when I have no actions to take. Once again, I can't sit still. I refuse to.

Waiting makes me restless. I keep checking my inbox, hitting refresh, waiting for some indication that things are moving forward. I fidget, I get up and walk around, I pour myself more coffee. And more coffee.

What I need is a distraction. Something to take my mind off the waiting. And there are plenty of options. Because we live in a world of diversion. What are our phones, devices, and screens, but an unending diversion?

Recently I drove through an extremely remote town in central Mexico on a surf trip. We passed these gorgeous coves and beaches, these beautiful little towns and villages, and every time, in the very center of town all the children of the village would be huddled together around a meager Wi-Fi signal, swiping down on their screens, hoping their Facebook or Instagram feed would refresh. Around the world, even in remote Mexican villages, technology has only aided our ability to divert our attention away from our restlessness.

This restlessness in our hearts has been called so many things over the years. Søren Kierkegaard calls it despair and makes the connection between it and what Scripture calls the sickness unto death. The wonderful writer Walker Percy refers to it as malaise. Brené Brown defines it as disconnection and "the lonely feeling."

Blaise Pascal, in *Pensees*, says, "Nothing is so insufferable to man as to be completely at rest, without passions, without business, without diversion, without study. He then feels his nothingness, his forlornness, his insufficiency, his dependence, his weakness, his emptiness."

Pascal goes on to describe the various ways that we will avoid this nothingness . . . fooling ourselves or diverting away our attention.

He talks about chasing rabbits as a demonstration of the futility of the distraction. In order for it to work, we have to believe that catching the rabbit will fulfill our sense of despair. But the fact is, we could just go down to the store and buy a rabbit. No, it is the chase that is important, and for it to work, we have to all buy in.

We are, as T. S. Eliot wrote, "distracted from distraction by distraction."

But in today's world, we've used technology to rid ourselves of waiting. We've all but done away with delay. Everything is on demand. No longer do we wait a week for the next episode of a TV show. We don't have to wait until the scheduled time of day for it to play. We don't even have to sit through the commercials. Instead, we plow through eight episodes at once. We binge.

No longer do we fast forward or rewind audio or video tapes. We don't flip over records from side A to side B. We don't even have to lug around a case full of CDs. Everything just magically downloads whenever we want it. And yet it still can't come fast enough.

As speeds increase, so do expectancies, and at a disproportionate rate. The faster we get, the more intense the frustration of waiting. Those things that eliminated delay only served to raise the expectations higher. The frustration level remains the same, but our tolerance for it has greatly diminished.

It takes just the slightest bit of traffic now to throw me into a funk. So I am constantly looking for shortcuts. Living in Laguna Beach, we have horrible summer traffic. Sometimes it is quicker to simply park and walk. But anyone who has lived here long enough has found ways around the busy stretches. We know how to jump the fences or maneuver down the back alleyways. The side streets can save you an easy fifteen or twenty minutes on what should otherwise be a five-minute drive.

But some days the traffic is inescapable. The shortcuts too are bumper to bumper. And as we sit in the unavoidable delays, our blood starts to boil. And we slowly become aware of the restlessness that is lurking in us. Something deep. That part of us that can't sit still. That won't sit still.

The waiting can be like an unwanted mirror for my thoughts. And as they come into view, I see them for all their embarrassing detail. I want to delete them like I'd delete a bad photograph. There are places in my heart that I'd rather not see. Waiting exposes the restlessness of my soul's ongoing attempts to avoid these areas of woundedness.

So often they come as questions, directed pointedly to my insecurities. "What a disappointment you are" or "Why would you think anyone would be interested in what you have to say?" Or, "Once they get to know you, they won't want you."

That one sticks. Because there are open wounds for that thought to conveniently latch on to. All it need say in its defense is "Remember?" Remember that time you were left for another? Remember that time you were overlooked? Remember that time you were misunderstood and undervalued and cast aside? Yes, yes I do.

I do remember. The memories are all too familiar. They've been playing on a loop down there, below the surface. These memories play like a terrible song on repeat, growing and morphing until the distortions become reality. Somewhere along the line they become our truth. And whether we know it or not, they are continually doing their damage, subtly, or not so subtly. Emotional pain or depression, physical pain and stress, crippling anxiety or insecurity . . . all of these can be manifestations of this inner sickness. A sickness unto death.

Waiting causes this inner turbulence to bubble up to the surface. It is the thing behind the thing. These thoughts are the sinister roots of the rocks and weeds in the soil of our lives. Our frenetic living and constant diversions are like hacking away at dandelions with a weed whacker. It might look contained or in control, but just wait till next week. Those weeds will be back and with a vengeance.

As we sit in the silence, as we wait, we are confronted with our helplessness. Our veneers and façades slowly fade. We lose composure and are forced to accept the fact that we are helpless. No matter of will can fully keep them at bay. The deeper belonging and peace we need is nothing. It is beyond our control. It is beyond circumstance and possession. It is beyond any relational gratification.

Pascal uses a king as the ultimate example of the unattainability of contentment and peace through material gain. He notes that when even the king, who has everything the world can offer, requires a jester to distract him from life, the rest of us are in trouble.

As a pastor in Laguna Beach, I've had plenty of time to reflect on this bizarre reality. Friends visiting from out of town will often say something like, "Wow, Jeff! I guess rich people need Jesus too." But the implication of their statement seems to include, "You sure picked an easy assignment." In Laguna, you're surrounded by comfort, affluence, beauty, luxury, and play.

I remember listening to N. T. Wright share at a nearby church and comically ask, "Why would you guys even need heaven? You're already living in it." Now he said this with a wink, but the truth is, if this is heaven, then we are in trouble. Laguna is one of the most anxious, depressed, and medicated places in the world. The suicide rate at our local high school is one of the highest in the nation.

Before I was the lead pastor at my church, I was the youth pastor. I used to tell the kids that they are a step ahead of where the rest of the kids in this world are, because those kids all think that if they lived where you live, if they just had what you have, then they would be happy. And you know this simply isn't true. Their Instagram accounts might pretend to be living the dream, but they are as desperate or even more desperate to numb the glaring pain in their souls.

And the more you see it, the more aware you are of it, the worse the pain.

In *The Sickness unto Death*, Kierkegaard says, "With every increase in the degree of consciousness, and in proportion to that increase, the intensity of despair increases: the more consciousness the more intense the despair."

The only way forward is to enter into the painful silence with courage and vulnerability. To listen. To release. To accept. To allow ourselves to be seen by God and by others for who we really are. Broken, helpless, and needy.

This means laying aside the distractions, the control, the numbing medications, the intoxicating feelings of being needed or included, and accepting the fact that the next thing will never be enough. It means stopping ourselves from the endless scrolling through Facebook or Instagram. Catching ourselves in that mindless loop and having the courage to ask our heart the deeper question, "What am I searching for? What is the longing or fear behind the need for distraction and diversion?"

We might very well catch the rabbit, but it will never give us what we are counting on it to provide. Peace and contentment never come this way. There is no prize big enough to satisfy our soul.

Beneath our impatience lies a heart that is restless and despairing. But beneath that is a longing deeper still. To be both seen and loved for who we are.

In *The Meaning of Marriage*, Tim Keller writes,

> To be loved but not known is comforting but superficial. To be known and not loved is our greatest fear. But to be fully known and truly loved is, well, a lot like being loved by God. It is what we need more than anything. It liberates us from pretense, humbles us out of our self-righteousness, and fortifies us for any difficulty life can throw at us.

Now I don't know about you, but this kind of vulnerability I find terrifying. As much as I may long to be fully known, it is also excruciating. I don't think any of us are able to completely drop our guard. I don't think our fragile hearts could take that kind of exposure.

As much as I long to be seen, I equally desire to go unnoticed. It creates a constant tension. As much as I may fantasize about the spotlight, I am also terrified of it. I want to be recognized but hate to be called on. I want to be special, but hate to stand out.

I remember one Halloween a coworker dressed up as me. Everyone thought it was hilarious. He had on one of my sweaters, was carrying my mug, wore a terrible wig, and did his best to mimic all my mannerisms. I was horrified.

A friend at the party offhandedly commented, "I think that is so cool, Jeff. You're iconic." I can understand how that could easily be one's response. But it wasn't mine. I felt naked and exposed. I wanted to disappear.

And I tend to think of myself as someone with a pretty good self-image and sense of humor. I like who I am, and even enjoy feeling unique and different. And yet, deep down, I worry about what others think of me. Much more than I care to admit. I'm afraid that maybe I'm the reason that everyone is laughing. That I'm the joke and everyone is just too polite to let me in on it.

There is shame down there. Embarrassment. Rejection too. And I mask it. And I convince myself that it is masked.

I remember an argument between Patty and me in which I caught myself before I said something I would regret. "Just say it," Patty said, but with kindness in her voice. I shook my head. "Why not?" she asked. "Because I don't want you to see this side of my heart. I don't want you to know what a bad person I can be." Patty just smiled and said, "Jeff, I already see it."

Of course she was right. You don't live with someone for over fifteen years and not see it. But I liked the idea that somehow I was able to hide the worst of me from her. Maybe then she would continue to love me. Maybe that way she wouldn't leave.

I remember feeling so exposed. Embarrassed, and at the same time, enormously relieved. Because I could see the look of love and acceptance on her face. Under the embarrassment was something more than I could hope for. True acceptance. And as painful and costly as it might be, there was nothing I wanted more.

And yet Patty's love is not deep enough to fill the well of my heart. Marriage is a wonderful symbol of unconditional love, and yet it will always remain imperfect, limited by our humanness, by our weaknesses, and by our love for self. Marriage teaches us to love, but only God's love can truly blanket us with the grace that will set us free.

Kierkegaard says this in *The Sickness unto Death*: "What is decisive is that with God everything is possible . . . but the critical decision does not come until a person is brought to his extremity, when, humanly speaking, there is no possibility. Then the question is whether he will believe that for God everything is possible."

It happens when we've run out of actions to perform. When we have used up all our available options. When we find ourselves to be powerless.

It is humiliating to our ego. We will do anything to avoid it. Which is why God guides us into these moments of helplessness.

And this is where faith comes in. To lay our hearts bare before God. To stop hiding from him and clothing ourselves with leaves. To allow him to see the places in us we are ashamed of, the wounds and sores. And to quietly, patiently receive God's healing touch.

FOR REFLECTION AND CONVERSATION

1. How do you relate to feelings of impatience? What do you do to distract yourself from your inner restlessness?

2. What would it be like to choose the longest line at the checkout or to drive in the slow lane? What would it cost you?

3. What is it about stillness that feels so threatening? What does waiting reveal to us about our own hearts?

4. Take an hour to sit quietly with God and reflect on the state of your own heart. Where are your levels of anxiety and stress? What is it like to sit with God with a heart wide open?

7

THE DESIRE
TO BELONG

I'M ALWAYS A BIT TERRIFIED WHEN I DO WEDDINGS. Something about the ceremony and formality of it all, the cameras rolling, the potential that any mistake I make will be viewed repeatedly for years to come. Not to mention the enormous expectations placed on you by the bride and groom, the parents, the friends, the family. It's a big day, and there is so much pressure to get it right.

But it is also a wonderful opportunity. What a diverse assortment of people gathered together around something universally beautiful. We are celebrating unconditional love. Whether or not you ascribe to a spiritual tradition, most people can suspend their differences and latch on to the beauty of the moment.

I just finished a wedding in Santa Barbara. It took place in a park overlooking the ocean. It was majestic. The backdrop of old oaks, the gleam of the sun off the sea, and a cool ocean breeze made for a delightful ambiance. The ceremony went smoothly, and as the bridal party began to exit to a familiar Jack Johnson tune, I breathed a sigh of relief.

It isn't that I'm desiring for the ceremony to be over. Not at all. It is more that the joy comes in the completion of a job well done. Before I pointed everyone up to the grassy area for cocktails, I paused for a blessing. "May God make his face to shine upon you and give you peace."

I found Patty and quickly searched her eyes to make sure it went well. She's my true test. That quick flash of pride in her eyes was all I needed to know. Whew! I could relax.

As we walked up to the grassy area, people slowly wandered over to shake my hand. I thanked them for their kind words. It was truly my pleasure.

And then a man stepped forward and, unlike the others, started with a disclaimer. "I wanted to let you know that I'm no longer a Christian. But something about what you said up there hit just the right tone. Thank you so much for the spirit of your words."

As I shook his hand, I could feel the stinging of tears in my eyes. A simple compliment, and yet something about this was different. It resonated on a level the others hadn't reached. This wasn't about my performance or content. It stirred something deeper. It was about my calling. It wasn't just emotion in my eyes; it was that familiar leap of the heart. His words meant something much deeper to me.

I had learned from Frederick Buechner to pay attention to "unexpected tears." He writes in *Listening to Your Life,* "More often than not God is speaking to you through them of the mystery of where you have come from and is summoning you to where, if your soul is to be saved, you should go next." But where was I supposed to go next? I'm still not sure of the answer to that. But this man I was speaking to was clearly on a journey. And in his mind, he had left the place I represented, his former faith, and yet found something still resonating in it even after he had left.

I mentioned this to a friend at the wedding and he smiled and said, "Maybe he'll find his way back to his faith?"

I paused and said, "Maybe he never left."

The journey of the heart is continually pulling us further up and further in. There is an inner dissonance that comes from the questions that pull us toward the fringes. At what point have we gone too far? At what point is it impossible to turn back? We approach the deep end of the pool, but always with one toe touching the bottom and our lips just above water level. But at some point we are unable to touch and all we can do is swim. Like my friend Rob likes to say, "You can't unsee what you've seen." In other words, there is no going back.

As I returned home that night I found an email waiting for me. I didn't recognize the name and sure enough the writer introduced himself as a friend of friends. He'd read my most recent blog. He had some things he needed to say to me.

His concern was less about the content of my blog reflections and more an overall criticism of my quoted sources. He expressed displeasure that I'd referenced a noted entrepreneur but had failed to quote Jesus or the Bible. He pleaded with me to simply present God's truth . . . which I'm assuming meant quoting Scripture . . . exclusively. "You're a senior pastor!" he exclaimed with rebuke. Clearly, in his eyes, I wasn't measuring up.

Now I've received these sorts of reproofs before. And I recognize his language as my own first language. This was the approach to Scripture—and to knowing God—in the church of my youth. Anything extrabiblical is seen as suspect. It is secular, and therefore, untrustworthy. To quote outside authority, such as science or philosophy, can even suggest a weakness of belief. And open-mindedness appears as a lack of conviction or dangerous curiosity.

I stared at the letter with a nostalgic melancholy. This was no longer where I lived or belonged. Somewhere along the way I had left this behind. It wasn't that I had ever really chosen to step out of the circle or cross the boundary line. Instead, the line was being drawn behind me and I found myself standing on the outside of it. I was no longer in the circle of trust. That thought caught me off guard.

I was also brokenhearted at his dismissal of another I had quoted, Pádraig Ó Tuama, a brilliant peace worker, who he had judged and cast aside. "You quoted a known homosexual!" My blood boiled in defensiveness. Why do we do this? Broad sweeping statements of rejection of anyone we find a particular disagreement with, even when the disagreement is completely unrelated.

What he had done, in objectifying and dismissing this brilliant soul, left me feeling so violated. He had taken all the complexity and beauty of a human being and reduced it to the issue he considered intolerable. The effect of his words was repulsive to me. It felt like Christianity at its worst.

I recognized very little of Jesus in the judgmental tone of the email—self-righteous, dismissive, arrogant, holier than thou. One of the very things I love about Jesus is his complete intolerance for this tone of voice. He comes straight at it. He overturns their tables. He refuses to be baited by their elaborate schemes. He instead brilliantly points them to the issue behind the issue.

I didn't respond. I know better. I deleted the email. But inside, my head and heart started to spin. Maybe the tears that had come when speaking with the guy at the wedding were somehow connected not just to his journey, but to mine. Maybe I was the one who had left. Maybe I am the one standing on the outside looking in. Maybe the compliment at the wedding was from one traveler recognizing one of his own.

I wish that judgmental tone were somehow an anomaly or exception to the rule for the church. But as I listen to the current climate of discussion on so many fronts, this is the tone I am hearing from huge swaths of the church-going population. Self-preservation, self-protection, self-preference. In the name of truth. Or orthodoxy. Or tradition. Or simply the way it used to be.

It's defending a place or position where I once belonged, but no longer feel that I do. I miss it, at least to some extent. But what I miss is not the place. I miss the feeling of belonging. I realize now that as my eyes filled with tears talking to the man at the wedding who had left Christianity, it was much more than just sympathy. It was empathy. I recognized myself in his story.

And yet I've never left my faith. This is important for me to make clear. Over the years, from my perspective, I've only grown deeper in my Christian convictions. My language has changed, but not the deeper meaning. The difference is much more in how the truth is held . . . what the words mean to me. My convictions and beliefs matter more today than they ever did. The differences of my opinions or the changes in my faith are much more related to how I choose to live than to scrutinizing the specific points of doctrine.

I do understand their concerns. But for me it isn't a difference of what we know to be true. Instead, it falls into the discipline of epistemology: how we know what we know. And the danger I see is when the ultimate end of increased knowledge is something more than the mere truth. Instead, the end goal can mistakenly become certainty. Indubitable knowledge. It becomes a quest to find that unquestionable foundation, impenetrable to any doubts or disbelief. It is a project that was started hundreds of years ago by a philosopher, René Descartes, but one that continues to this day. If we can find the one self-evident truth and deductively build from there, the tower of our knowledge cannot topple.

This principle, called foundationalism, is still quite common today. But it rarely unites us, as was the intention of Descartes. Instead, it mostly just divides us. Rather than bringing harmony, the foundationalist project has become a tool for determining who is in and who is out based solely on which "unquestionable" foundation you choose.

It is important to realize that, religiously speaking, this foundation isn't limited only to Scripture. Religious experience can also be a foundation. So can church authority. Even miracles, saints, or a different holy text.

These foundations define our tribes. We are the ones who believe in Scripture. We are the ones who hear from God. We are the church where miracles happen. The true church is the one who correctly performs the sacraments in such and such a way.

And the foundationalists aren't just the traditional or more conservative camps. The progressive movement has its very own brand of this. We are the ones who care about social justice, who represent the true heart of Jesus in our tolerance, who extend equality with the right amount of generosity. And the subtle subtext reads . . . and you don't, so you're out of the circle.

One of my favorite essays written by C. S. Lewis is called "The Inner Ring." Lewis begins the essay with an illustration from *War and Peace*, in which a higher-ranking officer is hushed by one of lower rank who is speaking with their commanding officer. He realizes that although he outranks the officer, there is a different system of power at play. This man he outranks is in higher standing in the inner ring. His conclusion is that the strength and power of the inner ring supersedes rank or any other means of status.

Lewis gives the warning that we will all be tempted to live our lives based on attaining the influence and power of the inner ring. And this game to be included in society's inner rings is often the cause for good men doing bad things. Because the pressure to belong in this circle is inherently one of scarcity and compromise. And for those who end up succeeding in this game of being included, the end result is always futile. Lewis says,

> The desire to be inside the invisible line illustrates this rule. As long as you are governed by that desire you will never get what you want. You are trying to peel an onion: if you succeed there will be nothing left. Until you conquer the fear of being an outsider, an outsider you will remain.

An outsider. That is how I felt. Often it is how I still feel.

The person who stands just outside the ring is often accused of being wishy-washy or spineless. They are thought to be lukewarm. The one without conviction. The one who desires for their ears to be tickled. They are the double minded. The one who wishes we could all just get along.

I know because these accusations have become familiar. If they aren't verbalized explicitly, they are insinuated by a roll of the eyes. It isn't always meant derogatorily. Sometimes it is just their frustration that seemingly even the simplest questions are returned with confusingly complex answers. Their response is more impatience than accusation. "Jeff, I don't have time for this. . . . Just get to the point . . . yes or no?"

I remember a friend once quoting Tolkien in reference to one of my answers by saying "Ask not the elves for advice, because they will tell you both 'yes' and 'no.'" But though Tolkien's reference points to the wisdom of the elves, usually we aren't so complimentary to the one in the middle. What we'd like to say is, "Stop equivocating!"

Because don't we just love simple answers? They build confidence. It is Ockham's razor with a fallacious twist. The simple answer is the right answer, even when it overlooks significant details. And because of this, the razor can often be turned and used for great harm. The scalpel gets turned into a sword.

In Greek mythology, Procrustes makes beds perfectly to fit. He lays you down on his bed and then cuts off the part of your legs that hangs over. Ouch!

The term gets thrown out there in philosophical circles. "That response is procrustean." I wish I'd hear it more in religious circles. Because sometimes I think we're more than content to walk around with shorter legs.

And on the other hand, the truth tellers are the bold proclaimers. We admire their strong conviction. They shout their truths from the rooftops, from their Twitter feeds, through whatever medium is available to them. They pound pulpits. They speak in elevated tones. This brings with it an air of conviction, of certainty, and it is highly effective. It draws supporters in droves. It draws a tight circle around those that agree and clearly delineates those who don't.

I remember reading N. T. Wright talking about Scripture as pieces of a puzzle, and how we all have chosen what pieces to include in the particular arrangement we've constructed. But just as important as what pieces you've chosen to include, and the way you've put them together, are the pieces you've chosen not to include. The piles of pieces we've pushed to the side. All the verses that push the other way, that create tension and paradox.

In most of the disagreements I come across, both sides are asking very different questions that happen to be masked as the same question. Each is arguing a dissimilar value or defending a different principle that is veiled. It is the question behind the question. Both arguments are logical, but unfortunately their arcs never seem to intersect. They miss. So both sides just get louder and louder. And the winner is the one who drowns out the other.

But conversations like this are so difficult because we don't know how to listen. We are incapable of accurately stating the position of the other side to their satisfaction. We aren't able to list their strongest arguments, or to listen in a way that demonstrates a level of respect. Tone of voice is everything.

It is my view that it takes even more conviction to remain in the dividing space between two opposing positions than it does to simply pick a side. To stand in the gap between believers and unbelievers is scary. But this is not the sphere of agnosticism, as some would claim. It actually takes tremendous personal conviction to occupy this space. What we must realize is that truth spoken from a place of separation or disconnection only creates noise. Or worse, violence. We become a clanging gong.

To stand in the middle is to stand in the place of engagement. It is where we turn the other cheek. It is where we love those who are difficult to love. It is where we remain, even when we are persecuted. The middle place is not safe. It is not comfortable. But it is where the real work gets done. It is the place where the deepest love happens, where we love those who are hard to love—even our enemies.

To stand in the middle place of an argument is to directly take on the ministry of reconciliation. To not only resolve the tension, but to reunite the relational fractures that come as a result of all the world's vitriol.

But to do this, we must learn how to stand alone. We must sink deep roots that allow us to endure the rushing floods of criticism. We must learn to bend and not break. It is the lonely role of the peacemaker. But it is a role that the world so desperately needs. It is a role that the church so desperately needs. To stop drawing circles or playing the game of who is in and who is out. To stand in conviction, drink deeply, and remain.

FOR REFLECTION AND CONVERSATION

1. Have you ever experienced unexpected tears like Buechner describes? What did you hear God speaking through them?

2. Can you think of a time where you received a criticism that affected your feelings of belonging? What was it like to find yourself outside the circle? Has that experience continued to affect your life? In what ways?

3. When you think of your own inner ring, who is in and who is out? What defines the line? Do you naturally feel like you belong or do you see yourself on the outside with your nose to the glass?

4. How do we remain in a relationship where we feel we no longer are welcome or belong? How do we remain relationally engaged without it becoming unhealthy?

8

LIVING WITH
QUESTIONS

R ECENTLY I WAS INVITED TO AN interfaith prayer rally dealing
with the deep racial division felt in our nation and community.
My heart leapt at the invitation. The cause of racial reconciliation
has been an increasing burden, not only for church and society as a
whole, but my own individual heart as well. And I've been feeling
helpless on the matter: shamed by my own position of privilege,
cautious of differing political views around me, and well aware of
the triggers that so easily push these matters of disagreement into
the morass of further division and fracture.

Currently, we live in a religious and political climate that is frac-
tured and struggling to find unity in its diversity. It feels like no one
is listening to each other. Instead we see entrenchment, or, at the
very least, avoidance of anything that strikes us as threatening. As I
looked at this prayer rally, my heart said go. But my head, of course,
ran through every scenario that might create disruption, misunderstanding, or distrust within my own personal faith community. My
own fundamentalism was showing.

Avoidance and disengagement weren't just appealing alternatives. My
flight mechanism gets triggered. My instinct for survival quickly takes
precedence over my desires to move forward, to explore, and to grow.

I remember listening to Seth Godin speak on the difference between curiosity and fundamentalism and he asked the question,

"What is your initial response to a new idea? The curious ask, is it true? The fundamentalist asks whether a fact is acceptable to their faith before they explore it."

And while I hate the idea of things remaining stagnant, I equally hate the inner turmoil created by the looks of distrust from those I am responsible to care for. When members of my church feel unsafe as the result of my need to explore I immediately feel guilty. When my curiosity leads me beyond the accepted boundaries, I can feel a lingering feeling of shame.

But there is something deeper stirring within me. Something core to who I am. My heart beats for both authenticity and congruency. I've always wanted to know why, to explore further. I've always been wired to ask the questions nobody else wanted to ask. Part of my need to attend the meeting was simply to maintain my own integrity.

But the urgency isn't only internal. The brokenness of the world isn't just my own personal discomfort. I can't help but think of my family and the world my kids are inheriting. I have these three beautiful children that are going to have to manage this mess we've made, or failed to fix. For me to disengage from the growing division in the world feels like the worst kind of neglect. I *must* engage.

And so Patty and I went. Such a simple act, and yet it was filled with what felt like risk. I was the only one from my particular evangelical tribe present. As the clergy stood up, I, for maybe the first time in my life, was the minority. The six-foot-four white male evangelical without a robe in the front row. I kinda stood out.

But as I stood, my self-conscious heart was also filled with pride. I was proud to stand with these brothers and sisters of mine from all walks of faith. It was so moving.

And as I sat through the service, I chose to simply open my heart to receive. And I was met with the warmest embrace I've felt in a long time. Broken hearts, united in purpose, seeing beyond difference to that place of deep commonality. People speaking their truth in ways that were their own and yet could so easily coexist in the sea of love that embraced us all. It was powerful. It was simple. And my heart was filled.

It is a dangerous thing to explore new ideas. At least it can feel that way. As our hearts and minds are opened to new information, and new ways of seeing, the thoughts start spilling over into other, seemingly unrelated areas of our lives. Our religious views affect our political views, which affect our life goals and values, which affect how we parent our children . . . and on and on.

Again, I'm naturally curious. My brain is wired for exploration. It is one of the things that brings me to life. Certainty, on the other hand, has the reverse effect. It is stagnating. It is impenetrable. It refuses to be questioned. It insists on being right.

New ideas are dangerous. They have this tendency to spread. Questions refuse to be contained by our categories. It is a slippery slope. Pretty soon, everything feels like it is up for grabs.

Questioning can create a sort of panic as one question leads us to another. It feels like the whole world is unraveling or coming apart. Each question is tearing at the support structures and threatening the collapse of the entire edifice.

At moments like this, it can be tempting to run back to our safeties and the comforting reassurance of our tribes. We turn to the books that speak consolingly to our existing beliefs. We avoid the difficult questions and turn our critical eye toward those outside of our camp. This habit is so rooted in us that we don't even see ourselves do it.

New ideas take us outside of the safety of the garden walls. And if we're honest, this can lead to some pretty unsettling places. When we start deconstructing our belief structures, we risk losing control of them. Pretty soon the why question is pressing into areas we'd considered settled. It reminds me of Lewis's analogy of going to a dentist. He doesn't just stop with the tooth that is painful and needs fixing. He starts poking around at teeth that don't hurt. That we'd prefer he would just leave alone.

New ideas are disruptive. They are intrusive.

One of the difficulties of remaining in the middle position is that we are cut off from our tribal or cultural affirmations. What I mean is, if I'm wrestling with a particular doubt, it can be extremely reassuring to simply surround myself with people who affirm me that I don't need to be asking the hard questions. It allows me to recommit to my *beliefs*, even if my actual *belief* is eroding. Because I can commit to something I don't believe, but only for a short term. At some point, I'll need to recommit. And recommit again.

Groupthink is a short-term solution, and yet all of us have the potential of remaining in the place of safety and avoiding the cognitive dissonance of what is unfamiliar. It pulls on us with a sort of gravity or resistance.

The dangers at first are subtle. In fact, we can turn this sort of avoidance into a seeming virtue. There is a simple beauty in the statement, "God said it, I believe it, that settles it." There is a childish naiveté that we can mistake for a childlike faith.

But the danger of this sort of allegiance is that often it hides a double standard. Because we only admire these kinds of commitments when it is within our own tribe and when we are in agreement to the same authority. We mistakenly see our interpretations as God's unquestionable foundation of truth. And to blindly commit to obedience can appear the epitome of faith. But blind obedience to our current understanding of Scripture can lead, and has often led, to some pretty scary places.

The truth is, when our intellectual minds conflict with social pressure, the social usually wins out. This is called confirmation bias and the implications and effects of it are everywhere. Simply put, according to the *New Yorker* in "Why Facts Don't Change Our Minds," it is "the tendency people have to embrace information that supports their beliefs and reject information that contradicts them."

Certainly, this has an effect not only on how we interpret biblical texts, but also, which texts we choose to focus on. Every tribe has its hot button issues. While they may seem subtle or simple in Scripture, when our tribe places them front and center, then they become a matter of belonging and identity. They determine who is in and who is out.

Having been raised in the evangelical church, I've seen numerous issues come and go. Styles of worship, Christian versus secular music, gifts of the spirit, speaking in tongues, emergent church controversies, and on and on. At one time, each of these issues was a reason to split and divide a congregation. However, in ten years, what was once a matter of dire consequence is often diffused. What once felt essential becomes secondary or even tertiary. "How could we have been so foolish?"

But instead of learning from the past, we always simply replace the issue with another. We leave behind our differences over the validity of prophetic gifting to then focus our attention on same-sex marriage. And where you land on that issue then becomes the litmus test for whether or not you truly believe in the authority of Scripture.

In Romans, Paul addresses one of the hot button issues of his day: meat sacrificed to idols. This was one that threatened to split the early Christian church down the middle between Jew and Gentile. In fact, when Paul and James met to discuss the consequences of Gentiles being converted in Acts 15, James dug in his heels on this issue. It was almost as if they were negotiating a trade—"I'll give you circumcision, but we're keeping meat sacrificed to idols." And Paul agreed.

But while that appears to be the end of their discussion, it didn't stop Paul from later changing his mind on the issue. In his letter to the Romans, he tells them that it isn't, in fact, a sin, and advises them to follow their hearts on the issue (Romans 14:19-21). If it doesn't bother you, don't worry about it.

But then he sets one more condition, and it is an important one. If it bothers another, then, out of deference, abstain. Don't do it. By exercising your freedom in front of another who is "weaker" or maybe, "more sensitive," then your actions are wrong. The moral of the story seems to be, "Do no harm."

Now, I can only imagine James's response had he lived long enough to read this letter to the Romans. I imagine he would have torn his hair out. He may have taken all of Paul's existing letters and pulled them off the shelves. And yet, here it is, in Scripture. And I'm so glad it is.

So often we come to Scripture looking for the rules or the answers. And what it gives us, instead, is an example of believers navigating through the tensions and complexities of real life—the tensions created naturally from living in a diverse community. How do we coexist with disagreements? What about when they are what some might consider to be essential points of doctrine?

Paul's answer: With sensitivity. With deference. A quiet answer that turns away wrath.

In other words, we lay ourselves aside and consider the needs of the other as more important than our own. We respond with hearts that are vulnerable and engaged. We consider the person as more important than the idea. I think this is what Paul means when he warns us of the dangers of brilliant, truthful words without love . . . they are nothing. Without love, truth becomes noise.

He tells us instead that love is patient and kind. Period. It can be more, but it can never be less. If our words lack patience and kindness, then they are clamor and chaos. Discernment without generosity profits us nothing.

I love the story, in Mark 9:24, where the man cries out to Jesus, "I do believe. Help my unbelief." Somehow these two can coexist, belief and unbelief. They aren't mutually exclusive. You can believe something without certainty and still believe it. And in Jesus' opinion, this man's faith is enough. Because the opposite of faith isn't doubt, as Anne Lamott tells us in her book *Plan B*. It is certainty.

And it applies to so much more than just hot button issues. This sensitivity is foundational for evangelism. It is essential for our moments of both triumph and despair. Henri Nouwen writes in a letter to a student, "Jesus' invitation to 'lay down my life for others' has always meant more to me than any physical martyrdom. I have always heard these words as an invitation to make my own life struggles, my doubts, my hopes, my fears and my joys, my pains, and my moments of ecstasy available to others as a source of consolation and healing" (*Love, Henri*).

Did you get that? Our doubts and fears become a way of comforting others. Sometimes what people need isn't the correct answers or advice. What they need is empathy. They need us to admit that we might not understand, but that we're with them.

Attending that interfaith rally did cost me something. It probably didn't help that a picture appeared in the *Register* with my wife and I sitting front and center amid representatives of other faith traditions. It took a while for the concerns to finally reach me, trickling through multiple sources until they finally came to my attention. "What does this mean? Is Jeff wavering in his convictions?" No one actually voiced these concerns directly to me, but instead to other sympathetic listeners who passed on their concerns.

And part of me still squirms at this. I feel defensive and self-protective. Argumentative. Angry even. But this is all part of my journey, and theirs. And I'm realizing that a significant part of my role is not reacting to the discomfort in myself or others, but remaining in it. Giving myself the permission to question, and allowing others the freedom to question me right back. Living with the distrust as a natural component of growth. Pushing others and letting them push me. Being okay with not having it all figured out. Celebrating the uncertainty as confirmation that I'm growing. And not rushing ahead, but instead allowing it to do its work. Slowly dissolving the fears and giving me the courage to push forward into my own unbelief, with the assurance that truth is greater than my limited conceptions and isn't threatened by my questions or doubts or lack of certainty.

FOR REFLECTION OR CONVERSATION

1. Have you ever felt like you've had questions that weren't safe to ask? How did you discover which questions were off-limits to your tribe? How have those questions changed over time?

2. Can you think of a time when you asked a question that you knew was off-limits? What was it that compelled you? What made it worth the risk?

3. Do you have any burning questions today? What do you do with them? Do you have a place or relationship where you are safe to explore?

4. Sometimes it feels like sensitivity requires us to simply not ask. What would it require to ask our questions, but with sensitivity toward others? How could we create a safer space to explore new ideas without reacting aggressively toward each other?

PART 3

THE SLOW OPENING

THIS CROOKED PATH OF TRANSFORMATION is not accidental. It has been designed for us. It is the story we are living into. And "who can straighten what [God] has made crooked?" In other words, it is by design.

And it requires so much of us. Glory demands us to be courageous. And humility insists on vulnerability and authenticity. Both require us to live with our whole heart. In spring we begin to open up to the new ways of God. And this is my discovery: the heart is the whole thing, period. From it flow rivers of life. But also, in it is where the sickness lies in me.

God is growing and enlarging my heart and healing it at the same time. And this is the way of transformation. And the texture of transformation is freedom.

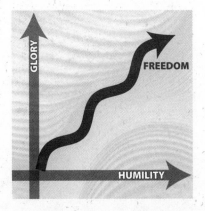

9

LEARNING TO BE ME

I USED TO FEEL SO NATURALLY IDEALISTIC and full of hope. It's one of the gifts of youth. There is such a beautiful energy and vision in that hope. This is one of the reasons I love working with young people. They are asking the questions of vocation not only with earnestness but optimism. They still see a blank canvas before them. Anything is possible.

But the truth is, this canvas will inevitably become marred with mistakes, frustrations, and failures. We unavoidably make the marks or strokes that we will regret. And slowly and painfully our perspectives shift. The optimism wanes. We become resigned to our fate.

Or maybe the opposite happens, but with a similar outcome. We achieve the things we were hoping to, only to realize they fail to deliver what they promised. Our hopes turn out to be misplaced. The longings for achievement are so often underpinned by a hidden hunger for praise or inclusion. And even when realized, their pleasure is fleeting and leaves us feeling like we're somehow back at the beginning.

The philosopher Martin Buber, in his wonderful book *Meetings*, writes about the completion of a lecture he gave at a young age on Ferdinand Lassalle to rousing applause. An old friend of Lassalle's, someone in his inner ring, came forward and grabbed Buber's hand and enthusiastically said, "Yes! Thus, thus he was!"

Buber felt tremendously confirmed. But shortly after that elation came fright. He saw his own impure heart revealed. He writes, "The true, hidden, cast aside, issue of my Lassalle studies revealed itself in a flash: the knowledge of the unmanageable contradiction that had burned in a bold and vain heart and out of it had been hurled into the human world." He stammered a thank you to the man and fled.

Buber's reaction came as a result of his own integrity and the startling exposure of the inauthenticity and selfishness the compliment had exposed in himself. As a young scholar, he realized that all he wanted was to get it right and to be seen as an equal among the academy. The contradiction in his own heart is that glimpse of ego, his own motives revealed. Even though he had gotten the speech right, at his core it was all about himself. It took success for him to see it with clarity, his heart intentions laid bare. He had gotten it right, and at the same time, profoundly wrong. He was an impostor.

Though his reaction to flee may appear severe, it reveals an inner level of transparency that most of us seek to avoid at all costs. His story is painfully honest. As I read it, I cannot help but see my own contradictions exposed. My own hidden motives become a bit more exposed.

I happen to have my own version of Buber's story—a moment of triumph that revealed the contradictions of my own heart. A victory that exposed my deep insecurities and shed light on old wounds still in need of healing.

You see, ever since junior high school, I've been convinced that there is something deeply flawed about me. I've been convinced that I am missing some key piece that everyone else possesses. It wasn't just some paranoid delusion. I could tell that I lacked the confidence, the quick wit, the aggressive gene that others around me seemed to possess and carry with such ease. It wasn't that I couldn't engage socially, but I always felt painfully self-aware that I was just one awkward comment away from that confused and disappointed look that meant I had failed to live up to their standard of cool.

And that insecure feeling settled in deep. It became part of my identity, from the music I listened to, to the company I kept. In one sense, I embraced that uniqueness. But not entirely. I wanted to be both normal and special. I still live in that tension. Hoping to be noticed and not noticed at the same time. For someone to value my "Jeffness" without noticing where I fail to measure up in other areas.

In order to cope with this social insecurity, I have developed a tendency to fly below the radar. I have taken comfort in investing myself in a small community and remaining in the same place over time in order to create some normalcy. Of course that isn't the only reason I've chosen a small community. I love it for all the depth of connection and intimacy that it offers. But it also offers familiarity and the opportunity to be truly known. To be valued for who I am, blemishes and all.

But every once in a while, I get asked to speak somewhere. And when I do, I feel the pressure of making a good first impression as well as my own inauthentic need to be impressive. Am I enough? Deep down, I'm convinced that I'm not. I become that scared junior high student all over again, fearful that I won't measure up.

But over time, I've learned to compensate for my areas of weakness. I've studied hard and read profusely, so that I can get around my lack of energy and emotional intensity by instead compensating by being deep and meaty. I have a good imagination and lots of curiosity, which allows me to look at things differently than most. The only problem is, the intellectual route can tend to leave the less bookish types feeling left out or even patronized. So all that heady stuff has to be balanced with some down-to-earth examples, and, of course, some good chunks of Scripture. Add some good humor to the mix and you've got a pretty good sermon.

But, in my mind, it's still not enough. I will always lack the dynamic presence of a high energy, type A, extroverted preacher.

I can fake it a bit, but it leaves me drained and feeling inauthentic. I cannot help but see myself at a disadvantage. The less preferred of the two.

This year I had a chance to speak at a large venue alongside another pastor I had listened to before. To me, he was everything that I was not. Tall, like me, but with a presence that filled the whole stage. He didn't need to earn trust or authority. He just claimed it. And he was so charismatic, everyone gladly gave him both.

My reaction was to shrink down a bit inside. I felt immediately judged and envious. He fits the definition and profile of successful leader and pastor that continues to cause me to feel inferior. This guy is who I'm "supposed to be." Except that I can't be like that. And honestly, I don't even want to be. It isn't that I wish I were different. I'm just saddened by what feels missing in me.

These are the tapes that play in my mind. Even more than insecurity is the feeling of sorrow that this is what people seem to value. All my self-pity is triggered and I start spiraling into my feelings of impending doom.

As I prepared my talks in the weeks leading up to camp, I remember feeling so inadequate. Ideas that had seemed fresh and interesting suddenly felt flat and boring. I could picture the audience rolling their eyes, or worse, nodding off. I met with my spiritual director, Lynn, and told her about my fears. What should I do?

Lynn looked at me with empathy and maybe a little pity. She knew this insecurity had been one of my lifelong companions. It was a well-worn road for her and me. I know too, that she saw how easily I could just remain there in that stuck place. Honestly, I almost preferred the sadness for the dysfunctional friend it had become. To be the overlooked genius was my preferred storyline. It was much better than really trying and failing. It felt safe.

Lynn said, "Jeff, just speak from your passion." My eyebrows raised. Passion? But I'm not that guy. Passion equals high energy. It requires rapid movement on stage without the use of a podium. It requires enormous hand gestures and brilliant comedic timing. It requires way too much confidence.

But she clarified: "Just speak from your heart."

"My emotions?" I asked.

"No, your passion."

I followed her advice. I chose topics that laid my heart bare. Stories where I wasn't the hero, but instead, the one on a journey, mistakes and all. I shared about my fears and weaknesses. I shared about my insecurity. I told them that God's power is perfected in our weakness. And I lived that message.

Each day, as I went through my talks with Patty, I was convinced that what I had prepared was rubbish. I felt like I was oversharing. But by the time I stood up to teach, I felt God's presence, and with it, authority. And it worked. People's hearts were touched.

There were several potential dissenting voices in the audience. A couple that had previously left my church. Several friends of others who had left as well. Faces that reminded me of the sting of rejection. But it didn't matter. In some ways, it was an opportunity I had always hoped for. To be able to excel in front of my detractors.

And the other speaker felt it as well. In fact, I could see his insecurity grow. I could hear his voice change. His topics shift. He even said, "I know I'm not the artist, theologian, like Jeff. . . ."

I think that, deep down, my ego longed for this scenario. And it got what it wanted. My reaction was a shock to me. In that moment of triumph, it felt empty and meaningless. Instead of feeling like I had won, simply playing this game felt like losing. It left me feeling sad.

I felt like Buber in his moment of accolade, seeing his own heart, and realizing just how counterfeit his intentions felt. Unlike him, I didn't flee. But it did leave me feeling deeply disoriented and a bit ashamed.

Not for the talks, or the opportunity, or the gift of finding my true voice and passion. But for all the wasted energy worrying about what was missing in me. About the areas I didn't measure up. About all the things in me I was tempted to hide or try to change. What a complete waste of time!

To watch someone else, someone I had insecurely compared myself to, exhibit similar fears and comparisons, was eye opening. It shouldn't have been. He was obviously the stronger one. Except that he wasn't. Neither of us was. We were both deeply broken, compensating for our wounds and areas of seeming deficiencies. Both of us felt inadequate.

The point can almost feel like a cliché. And yet, it was so helpful for me to see the futile spiral I was caught in. Win or lose, the whole game was entirely about ego. And the quickest way forward was to give up the whole game. This isn't at all how God keeps score. The metric we'd created was irrelevant.

But giving up the game costs us something we deeply value and cling to: the pleasure of superiority, the satisfaction of winning. It costs us the feelings of triumph.

Instead, these victorious feelings must be replaced with a sort of self-forgetfulness. We must give up both the pain of failure and the joy of victory and instead cling to the satisfaction of meaningful work, the savor of courage, and the deep joy of speaking vulnerably and authentically. There is a lightness to it. It feels like freedom.

When we let go of this need for praise and recognition, we are able to release the results. They aren't where our interest lies. It isn't what compels us.

I can imagine what that would be like. But that self-forgetfulness still feels a long way off.

The spring season is when we begin to catch a glimmer of hope. New life emerges, even if it is just a hint. And we begin to see the fruit of the work that has been taking place all along. Roots have grown deeper than we thought. The cold of winter is yielding its reward. And yet summer can remain some distance away.

It is a sobering realization that new growth only comes at great cost. It is out of seasons of suffering that new life begins. Only when we've weathered storms do we see more clearly.

It ages us, this cycle of growth. It steals away our naiveté and yet it need not be replaced with hardened callouses. When we've suffered well, we grow. When we die to self, we are reborn. When we give up the need to be right, often the truth is resurrected.

This is the pattern of transformation. Death and resurrection. The need for rebirth. "Unless a kernel of wheat falls to the ground and dies, it remains only a single seed. But if it dies, it produces many seeds" (John 12:24). Martin Buber calls this the resurrection of the right. And resurrection is the right word. In that process of death and rebirth comes something new and greater. It is transformation.

But the feelings of dying feel nothing like transformation. They feel like we're losing ourselves. Like we're wasting our precious time. Our efforts feel futile. We wonder if we're playing the fool.

The process of dying to self feels cold. It feels like we're going numb. And we wonder if we'll ever come out of it. It makes me want to quit. I begin to see greener grass everywhere I turn.

But "deep roots are not reached by the frost." That's what Bilbo's poem says. And I cling to the truthfulness of this statement in times of discouragement and despair. I have to believe that we can continue to grow through these winter freezes and not lose heart. But something in us must change if we aren't to wither on the vine. What if it is the frost that changes us? What if the frost is what we need?

The celebrated chef Dan Barber, in an interview with Krista Tippett, said,

> The best root vegetables have to go through intense freezes to get the sugar. To get the root vegetables that all of us adore, the beets and the parsnips and the celery root, the carrots, for sure,

these need to be stressed under several hard freezes. And, in fact, if stayed in the ground in the right soil with the right seeds, end up becoming carrots that far, far exceed in flavor, in sugar and in flavor, anything that's grown in a monoculture in those warmer climates. (*On Being*)

I couldn't help but think of Paul's teaching on the fruit of the Spirit. I love this metaphor for determining the eternal or kingdom quality of our actions. How does it taste to you?

But taste is so subjective. Just join my family for dinner. There is hardly a meal where everyone rejoices. Each of us prefers something different. We make meals that can be modified, where we can each prepare the meal in our own way. But even then, someone isn't quite happy. And often, my youngest and pickiest eater has to be reminded that she must at the very least try whatever is on her plate.

I think that many people process ideas like my daughter assesses her food. Not by how it tastes, but how it looks. She has extremely limited categories for what is acceptable. If it were up to her, she would just stick with the staples of eggs, cheese pizza, refried beans, and apples.

Sometimes pastoring feels like being a chef in a restaurant where everyone just wants to eat off the kids' menu. No one wants the ribeye. They just want chicken nuggets. Again. And again.

In 1 Corinthians 3:1-3, Paul writes,

Brothers and sisters, I could not address you as people who live by the Spirit but as people who are still worldly—mere infants in Christ. I gave you milk, not solid food, for you were not yet ready for it. Indeed, you are still not ready. You are still worldly. For since there is jealousy and quarreling among you, are you not worldly? Are you not acting like mere humans?

There is a wonderful movie, *Babette's Feast*, where Babette, a world-class chef from Paris who has become a refugee among a village of poor fishermen, offers her benefactors a meal provided by a large inheritance check she has received. Her friends have found out about the money and are convinced she is going to leave them. Unbeknownst to them, Babette has spent the entire amount of inheritance on the feast she has prepared for them. The very best of everything.

And they miss it. They hardly taste it out of the consuming worry that they are going to be rejected and left by this woman they have grown to love. Their fear and anxiety has numbed their taste buds. They might as well have been eating frozen pizza.

In Psalm 57, as David writes from his place of hiding in the cave, he exclaims, "Awake, my soul!" Let me have eyes to see. Let me have ears to hear. And, just as importantly, let me have taste buds that taste. All of us need our senses to come alive. Our souls need to be awakened.

This requires us to be present. One of the most beautiful reminders about a feast is that it so quickly becomes a memory. Hours of preparation for a glimmer of joy. It's gone in an instant. If our minds and hearts are stuck looking forward or backward, we cannot savor the goodness of the immediate moment. And life itself loses its richness. Everything tastes like chicken or runny eggs.

Personally, I know of no other way to remain present than to practice intentional times of detachment. To practice Sabbath rest. To enter into silence. To slow down, sometimes to a snail's pace. To stop striving. To be still. To allow the lifeless branches to be pruned. To abide.

I'm speaking again this summer at Forest Home. Putting together a series of talks. As I do, I think back on that memory of last summer and see it as such a gift that continues to speak affirmation to my heart. Jeff, be yourself. Be true to who you are. Follow your passions. But most of all, stop measuring yourself according to the petty metrics of the world. Let go of the fear and worry that keep you small and stuck in your own head. Stay in that place of authenticity.

And savor the taste of freedom. The joy found only in the present moments. Stop living in that place of restless comparison and fleeting affirmations, and relish the deep work that God continues to do in my heart. And do my best to prepare for them the finest feast I know how . . . and let the rest go.

FOR REFLECTION AND CONVERSATION

1. Do you relate to the feeling of inner contradiction, where you are praised for something that, in your heart, you know is not true? How do you feel when you see this inner hypocrisy? How do you tend to respond?

2. When you compare yourself to others, how do you measure up? Where do you see yourself as deficient? What would you change about yourself if you could?

3. Can you relate to my feelings of emptiness when I came out on top? Have you had a similar experience? What are the false desires that were driving your need to compete? What can you learn about the things your heart actually was desiring?

4. Where might God be taking you deeper? How has the winter season prepared your heart for a deeper passion? How is God increasing your ability to taste and see?

10

THE SIGNIFICANCE
OF SMALL PRAYERS

S EVERAL YEARS AGO, MY SON earned straight As during his first semester of middle school. We weren't expecting it. He's smart and all, but he'd never come home with that strong of a report card. We were super proud. Best of all, so was he.

That little man beamed. He reached into his pocket to show me the awards card he'd received. It gave you discounts at all the best local Laguna Beach restaurants and retailers. Twenty percent off at the local surf shops as well as cheap burritos and tacos—everything a growing boy needs.

"Let me see it," I said encouragingly.

And then his face fell. He checked each pocket in turn and then rechecked. "Annnnd, I lost it," he said, trying to smile. Trying to act like he didn't really care.

I just remember my heart breaking. I know how that feels. Maybe a little too well. Deep disappointment coupled with embarrassment for having actually cared that much. Ashamed to have exposed that vulnerability that allows itself to delight in something so seemingly insignificant, and yet so tenderly important.

"Where do you think you lost it?"

"Probably up at the tennis court," he said. "There's no way it's still there. Oh well, I probably wouldn't have used it anyway."

I felt helpless. He was right. If he lost it up there, there is no way we'd find it. The courts aren't lit, it was pitch black outside, and besides that a thick fog had rolled in.

As I sat there feeling helpless, I felt another one of those nudges. It was as if God poked me in the ribs and said, "Go get it. . . . It's up there."

"Let's go find it," I said.

"Dad, there's no way. I don't even know if it is there."

"It is," I said, knowing full well I was only going to do more damage if we failed.

But I felt that strange peace. This wasn't me working out my own junk or trying to play God. It felt like obedience, and a personal step of faith.

As we walked to my truck, I shot a text to the elder board, letting them know I was going to be late. This was an emergency. We drove to the top of the hill and had to park out on the street since the parking lot was already chained off. It was spooky walking out there in the dense fog. It felt like a scene from *Hound of the Baskervilles*. I used my phone as a flashlight and Gabe used the little light I kept in the glove compartment of my truck. We walked out onto the court where he had his lesson that afternoon.

We looked everywhere. Under the benches, in every corner of the court, back and forth we swept and nothing. It wasn't there.

"I told you, dad."

What in the world?! This was way bigger than a little card, at this point. All of a sudden my own fears came clamoring in. Why would you do this, Jeff? Why would you let yourself care this much? There I was, this little boy trying to pretend he wasn't about to burst into tears.

"Well . . . it was worth a try."

We walked towards the exit of the court and he paused. Wait . . . this isn't the court. It's the next one over.

Both of us went running over to the low chain-link fence separating the two courts and practically hurdled it. We walked out onto the court and no joke, there it was sitting right in the middle of the court—a little gold card sitting alone there in the middle of all that green.

He walked over and picked it up, a bit embarrassed about the joy and relief he felt. That little heart restored, at least for today.

"God told me it was up here," I said.

"Really?"

"Yeah."

I wished so badly I could have had the courage to tell him that ahead of time. I knew it, but I didn't. I felt like that man who confessed to Jesus, "I do believe; help me overcome my unbelief!" (Mark 9:24).

We got into my truck and headed back. We walked back in and I quickly shared the story with Patty, gave her a kiss, and hurried to the meeting for which I was already thirty minutes late.

I walked in feeling a sense of peace. God was watching, listening, seeing the little details of my life and speaking into them.

As I entered the room it was dead silent. I sat down quietly, inquisitively looking around the room for a hint of what I had stepped into.

My friend was sharing some news involving his son. He was away at college and the only one home in his house when a roommate's friend had shot himself there. And this story came on the heels of several other heart-wrenching stories I knew that had taken place during the last semester, on top of some serious health concerns he had been dealing with.

I know this kid. He was in my youth group years ago when I had been the youth pastor. A bit challenging at times, but a heart of gold and a mind as quick and sharp as they come.

I had been walking in with a story to tell. All of a sudden, it felt so pathetic and small. Why in the world would God care about a stupid report card award? Why take the time to whisper about that when these events were unfolding?

I felt ashamed. Am I that "first world problems" kind of Christian who thanks God for parking spots opening up in front of me, when poverty and injustice rip the world apart just outside of my comfortable Orange County bubble? My exciting, self-congratulatory story felt grossly inadequate.

As we sat there in prayer, I didn't have the words. I just held this young man in my heart and mind. I prayed, "God, you somehow cared enough to send Gabe and me up to the tennis court to find his insignificant card. I can't believe that your priorities are that out of whack to have missed this. Please tell me you care more about this young man. Please tell me that somehow you are with him in the midst of the chaos and storm of this horrific day."

And God answered: "I am."

That's all I got. But somehow it was enough. Tears poured down and I found myself thanking God over and over for that moment on the tennis court. It was a sparrow falling to the ground. It was one of the hairs on my head. It was a lily in the field in all its splendor. "Look at the birds of the air; they do not sow or reap or store away in barns, and yet your heavenly Father feeds them. Are you not much more valuable than they?" (Matthew 6:26).

Faith is an awkward road to walk. It is understood looking backwards but lived forward, as Kierkegaard said. That means that each step is a risk. There are no guarantees, no formulas to count on. We cling to the moments of meaning and cohesiveness we've experienced and plunge into the unknown.

There is a haunting passage that C. S. Lewis writes in *A Grief Observed*. He says,

> When you are happy, so happy you have no sense of needing Him, so happy that you are tempted to feel His claims upon you as an interruption, if you remember yourself and turn to Him with gratitude and praise, you will be—or so it feels— welcomed with open arms. But go to Him when your need is

desperate, when all other help is vain, and what do you find? A door slammed in your face, and a sound of bolting and double bolting on the inside. After that, silence.

It reminds me of Isaiah writing, "Truly you are a God who has been hiding himself" (Isaiah 45:15).

That hiddenness can be excruciating. It is the shadow side of the glorious mysteries of God. It is Qohelet saying in Ecclesiastes, "Who can straighten what [God] has made crooked?" (Ecclesiastes 7:13).

But it isn't our place to make it straight. Instead, we cling to the little answers to prayer and trust that God is in the big ones.

The small act of compassion that God had for my son, that was for me. The apple of my eye. That dear little boy who was growing up so incredibly fast. To do that for him was the most tender gift God could have given to me.

"Jeff, I know you. I'm with you. Trust me."

He didn't actually say those words to me, but I heard them anyway. And I cling to them still.

FOR REFLECTION AND CONVERSATION

1. Have you ever had God answer a simple prayer? What was it like to receive that simple word or gentle nudge? How do you see God's heart in the small things?

2. Do you ever wrestle with the discrepancy between God's simple answers to prayer and the enormity of the pain and suffering in the world? How do you make sense with the discrepancy?

3. Assuming you are able to trust God in this situation, what is it that you hold on to? Where do you place your hope and trust? What should faith look like when we are wrestling?

11

TRUSTING GOD IN
THE BROKENNESS

THE YEAR 2017 MARKED THE thirtieth anniversary of U2's seminal album *The Joshua Tree*. When I first saw them perform it live, I was the age of my son. I wasn't old enough to drive. My youth pastor drove a bunch of us to the show for night number two at the Coliseum. The Pretenders were the opening band, but the Dalton Brothers opened before them. I remember the lead singer saying they only played two types of music, country and western. We practically booed them off the stage, only to find out the next day that it was U2 dressed up as cowboys, performing Hank Williams songs for their own amusement.

That night was like a rite of passage. My heart soared. That red-orange screen as the band entered is still emblazoned in my mind. I remember the chorus of thousands of people singing every word to every song. It was a church choir like I'd never experienced before.

There was already so much significance tied to this band for me. *War* was the first album I ever purchased—on vinyl—from a Christian bookstore. To all those raised evangelical, you might remember those concerned arguments about whether or not U2 was a "Christian band." As silly as that question might appear today, it really seemed to matter at the time. Now it just makes me cringe.

When *The Joshua Tree* came out, it never left my tape deck in my VW bus for that whole year. I loved every single song. But, if I'm honest, there was that one song that caused me a bit of angst: "I Still Haven't Found What I'm Looking For." Bono calls it a gospel song with a restless spirit. That one song worked in my heart like a splinter.

[You] carried the cross of my shame,
But I still haven't found
What I'm looking for.

At first, I remember feeling confused. What did he mean, he hasn't found what he's looking for? Isn't Jesus enough? I felt abandoned. I clung to songs like "40" and "Sunday Bloody Sunday" as anthems of my own faith. But for Bono to express such seeming dissatisfaction with his faith, to admit he was still searching, left me brokenhearted. I had lost my standard bearer.

But the chorus of that song wouldn't leave me alone. It was so brutally honest. It put its finger right on my own wound. It touched the question I was trying not to ask. "Is this it? Is this enough? Is this all there is?" Sunday school had taught me not only the right answers, but that it broke the rules to even verbalize such questions. Doubts signified disbelief, and underneath them a lack of faith. If Jesus wasn't enough, then you were doing something wrong. You were the problem.

But over the years, the courage behind those lyrics gave me the freedom to admit that Bono's questions were often my own. That the simple formulas, three point sermons, and evangelistic tracts left me feeling less certain, not more. The more I insisted on being right, the less confident I felt.

The cracks in my faith were widening. I'd seen too many leaders fall. Too many wounds given in the name of love. Too many unanswered prayers. And in a world with such brokenness, the simple answers became embarrassingly small. It had to be bigger than all of this, right?

Yet my core beliefs felt unchanged. As others looked on my doubts and questions with concern and even suspicion, my heart cried out, with Bono's, "You know I believe it." Like that father blurting out to Jesus, "I do believe; help me overcome my unbelief!" (Mark 9:24).

Thirty years later, as news of another Joshua Tree tour was announced, I had decided I wasn't going. Ticket prices are always depressingly high, and in this crazy world we live in, I'm growing more and more reticent about taking part in large public gatherings. But my friend James offered tickets at the last minute, and I jumped at the opportunity. I was there at the beginning. Somehow I knew I needed to be there now.

These songs, like Bono said that night, are more the fans' songs than theirs. That certainly rang true for me. And this concert did something for my heart that all their shows in between hadn't. At that first Joshua Tree concert, something was stirred in me. And now, thirty years later, I realize that it is still stirring.

As U2 came on stage, Larry began that familiar drum cadence of Sunday Bloody Sunday, followed by Edge's guitar riff (the "stairway to heaven" for the guitar players of my generation), and a single spotlight illuminated each member of the band.

I can't believe the news today
I can't close my eyes and make it go away.

As they walked out, my eyes started pouring tears, embarrassingly, salty stinging tears that kept me from seeing clearly. I tried in vain to wipe them away.

All these years later, the questions still remain, and my answers feel even less clear than they did. The doubts have changed and deepened, moving me outward toward something more. But I'm learning to make peace with the questions and doubts, to not force the answers that continue to elude me, and to trust that everything will be answered in its proper time.

Thirty years later, I have learned to live and remain in this in between desert place. In this gap between salvation and redemption. I am still learning it. I am still running.

The poet Rainer Maria Rilke says in *Letters to a Young Poet*, "Live the questions now. Perhaps you will then gradually without noticing it, live along some distant day into the answer."

And the answers lie in the longings. Those longings tell me that we are made for something more. That the yearnings for justice, love, and mercy will ultimately prevail. And what I believe, and know in my heart, is that we're being drawn toward it. Toward what C. S. Lewis calls, in "The Weight of Glory," the echo of a tune that we have not yet heard.

Sometimes the church has been accused of being so heavenly minded that it is of no earthly good. But on this evening, the concerns and conflicts in the world weren't set aside. They remained front and center: the political conflicts, the battles for equal rights, the refugee crisis, the fight against AIDS. In the midst of the world's brokenness came a call to engage. To not look the other way. To act.

Leaving that night, I felt something stirring again. In the midst of a world that is so broken and filled with pain, and hurt, and evil, I felt caught up in the truth and beauty and power of love casting out fear. Light can overcome darkness. Mercy will triumph over judgement. All things can be made new. Once again, I felt hope.

As a pastor, to admit that I still haven't found what I'm looking for feels like a dangerous admission. Because the expectation of pastors is that we, of all people, have indeed found what we're looking for. Expressions of doubt and discontent aren't just troubling to a congregation, they are a lousy sales pitch. A lack of certainty feels like a lack of belief.

Successful preaching is about answers, not questions. It is about reaffirming, not deconstructing. We come to church to have our faith bolstered up, not challenged or pushed.

It is a hard time to be a pastor. I just read about a recent shooting in a Baptist church in Texas. I don't even know what to say. My heart is so heavy and broken and discouraged. But when I go to my church, people are waiting for comfort. That everything is going to be alright. We are so bad at mourning. We refuse to lament.

I wonder if the questions underneath are too frightening. We've created these elaborate coping mechanisms of faith in order to keep things simple, but it requires enormous effort to keep our blinders up. At some point, you are forced to cover your eyes and ears.

One Sunday when I was feeling particularly burdened, a parishioner came up afterwards with a gentle rebuke. "Jeff, we're counting on you to have joy. We need you to be the one to hold it together. To have hope."

And to a certain extent, I get that. One of the pastor's roles is to see beyond the storm clouds. To point to a greater reality that draws us beyond our circumstances. Again, to repent is to see beyond.

And I would readily agree that the pulpit is not the place for therapy. Pastors need to avoid working out their emotional baggage in front of the congregation. Vulnerability is an important value, but not one appropriate to model on a Sunday morning. But humble transparency is critical and without it, we put forth a dangerous image of something unattainable. Because that plastic image of myself doesn't actually exist. It is the false self. And like Merton tells us, God doesn't love that person because he doesn't know that person.

It is a fine line between managing our emotions and being inauthentic about our emotions. But it is a line we must look for and seek to draw closer to.

And, as a pastor, while my congregants may prefer sermons and messages filled with boldness and certainty, this might not be what they need—what any of us need right now. Could it be that the more powerful sermon is not the one that insists on being right, but instead the one that puts its finger on the actual wound and asks why? That admits that things don't always make sense? That acknowledges that faith is messier than we'd like it to be?

I think of the story in the Gospels where Jesus is asleep in the boat in the middle of a squall. The disciples are at the end of their rope and, in Mark's version of the story, they shout out the question at Jesus, "Are you going to let us drown?" As I read that story, I am so glad to have that piece of information included. We sense that they are scared, overwhelmed, but also angry and a bit baffled. "Are you seriously sleeping?!"

Sometimes I feel the exact same way. I pray and pray for someone who is sick that doesn't get well, and I think, "God, you are blowing it right now! This one is a no-brainer!" I'm at my wit's end. And God seems to be content to just sleep.

Jesus does give them a bit of a rebuke of their faith. But he also demonstrates a level of power and authority that they could barely comprehend. He makes the wind and the waves go completely still. They hadn't even thought of praying for that. They just wanted the boat to stay afloat.

And instead of answering their doubtful question, he demonstrates a power and control that creates calm and stillness. His response—trust me. In your unfulfilled longings, in your insecurities and doubts, in your unresolved complaints. Trust me that I'm taking you further than your world of certainty and control can contain. And above all remember that I go there with you.

FOR REFLECTION AND CONVERSATION

1. Is there a time when you experienced cracks in your own faith? What was it like to experience doubt? What was the response of others to your concerns?

2. Are you able to identify the longing underneath your questions? How have these longings shaped your spiritual journey? How have they caused your ideas and perception to grow and change?

3. How do you feel about the messiness or mysteries of faith? Are there questions that God isn't answering? Where are you being asked to simply trust?

12

THE SLOW WORK
OF THE CROSS

I WAS SPENDING A QUIET DAY at the Getty. Over the last few years I've had a rhythm of spending one day a month in silence. The Getty is a marvelous place to go to get out of my head and listen for God's voice. It is spacious and filled with beauty. The regular pieces are some of my very favorites and there are all sorts of little nooks to sit and reflect and be still.

I am, like so many, drawn most to Van Gogh. So many times I've sat in front of his irises and marveled at their beauty and color. But this day I kept moving around the room toward the impressionists. I have always loved Monet as well, and as I stood before his painting of the ships I felt God nudge me to look closer. What was it about this painting that I liked so much? I could feel that something was in this for me today.

The colors are dark and murky. There is a sort of melancholy in it. But what I love so much about Monet is the uncompleted quality to it. As I read the description, it turns out that this painting in particular was strongly rejected by the academy at that time. They called it an unfinished painting. And I knew they were somehow accusing me of the same thing.

My style has always been unpolished. Rarely do I teach deductively. I prefer an inductive style that can maneuver from point to point with the same freedom I enjoy in exploring new ideas. I love to follow an idea down the rabbit hole.

It drove my homiletics professor batty. He wanted three point sermons each with three supporting points. I would always bristle at that deductive style of teaching. It felt like presenting theology as a geometric proof. It felt like I was putting deep mystery into a box that diminished its elegance. I couldn't do it.

I quoted him Marshall McLuhan, that "the medium was the message." That the structure was actually working against the wonder and depth. I wasn't trying to be argumentative. I still believe that the very structure sets the entire tone.

It reminds me of a former pastor, back when I was a youth pastor, who would print his sermon points in the bulletin with one-word blanks to fill in. I would catch the students filling in the answers before he started speaking and then grading themselves afterward on how many answers they had gotten right. That sounds so cynical now, and I promise that I told them not to do it, but deep down it was hard to blame them. The format of the notes itself took deep truth and oversimplified it down into a form that felt cliché.

I told my professor that I felt the format we were being taught suggested a more reductionist view of spiritual truth than I could teach with integrity. It felt like vivisection, which is incredibly helpful for learning, but kills the specimen in the process. We might better understand the frog's anatomy, but he could no longer jump or croak. Similarly, we might grasp theological truths, but in a way that left them sterile and almost lifeless. They leave us with a sense that we've somehow figured it out.

Teaching is so valuable, and I love those that can boil down complexity to terms that can provide greater understanding and clarity. But sometimes I feel like we've intentionally avoided the mystery because it is messier than we'd like. This reduction of truth might bring a level of satisfaction, but we must not mistake that for enlightenment.

My professor just shook his head at me. "Well, I'll tell you this much. You'll never preach on television."

As I stared at the Monet, I felt such affirmation. Not that my sermons have Monet's level of brilliance and artistic giftedness. But the beauty of the unfinished work brought so much deep affirmation. In the blurry impressions there was such raw emotion. In the lack of precision and clarity was the space to see through and beyond. Mystery was not something to be grasped, but instead a force that pulled us further and further in.

Spiritual growth is necessarily slow work. It requires us to till the soil of our hearts, to wait patiently for the roots to grow deep, and to wait patiently until the fruit has ripened to its fullest and most flavorful. It other words, it takes time. It takes a lifetime. And without vision and hope, the waiting can be unbearable.

Fast food works because the line moves quickly, the food is cheap, and afterwards we feel full. Mission accomplished. Except that the food does little for our actual health and instead leads to all sorts of health concerns such as obesity, heart and cholesterol issues, digestive problems, and on and on.

We figured out ways to shortcut the process. To boil the gospel down to four simple laws and a prayer. We've created ways to streamline spiritual growth, checking boxes along the way. But the costs of these shortcuts to spiritual fruit are a loss of taste and nutritional value. The sad thing is that for most of us, it is a price we're willing to pay. The immediacy of the feelings of comfort and peace is enough. Actually healing from our wounds, recovering and being made whole, becomes secondary.

We've reduced discipleship down to a conversion story, a class on the basics of faith, a spiritual gifts test, perhaps, and extra credit for those who join a small group, and for those who find a service opportunity in the church.

In our world, impatience reigns. Efficiency has become the chief end of man. And the compromises are becoming clear. We have sacrificed the very essence of what we are truly seeking. We have settled for comfort instead of holiness. The real work of the gospel, bringing us together in love, has been exchanged for belonging to a tribe. The checklist brings the assurance that we are "in."

The church has fallen in love with quick results. We want powerful conversions and radical healings. We want passionate, dynamic worship. We pray for something new, something larger, more revival. These move us, they impress us, and they don't cost much.

I was recently listening to a talk by Jennifer Roberts, an art historian from Harvard, speak on the deceleration in learning. She said, "Every external pressure, social and technological, is pushing students in the other direction, toward immediacy, rapidity, and spontaneity—and against this other kind of opportunity. I want to give them the permission and the structures to slow down" (Harvard Initiative for Learning and Teaching 2013 conference).

Roberts has her students sit for three hours with a painting and just observe. According to the students, it ends up being one of the most difficult of all their assignments. To sit and look intently. To delve beneath the surface. To notice the subtleties, the intricacies, the artist's hidden intentions. There is simply no way to speed up the process. To properly view a painting requires time, and focus. It takes patience.

Roberts goes on to say, "It serves as a master lesson in the value of critical attention, patient investigation, and skepticism about immediate surface appearances. I can think of few skills that are more important in academic or civic life in the twenty-first century."

And I would add to her list, spiritual life. In fact, I'd put that one at the top. The path of wisdom requires not just time, but patience, curiosity, and attention to the depths and the complexities it reveals.

This is the way of wisdom. In his well-known prayer, Pierre Teilhard de Chardin writes, "Above all, trust in the slow work of God." I love that prayer. Because it is the slow work that remains. This is the growth that endures.

I have been studying Luke's Gospel, and have enjoyed his inclusion of several characters in the early chapters that enter and then exit quickly from the birth story of Christ. Two of these, Simeon and Anna, are found in Luke 2. They are both in the winter season of their lives and both of them have been waiting and waiting for peace and consolation for Israel.

Simeon was promised by the Spirit that he would see the Messiah, and sure enough, he is led by the Spirit to the temple as Joseph and Mary arrive. Simeon gets to cradle the baby in his arms, who is less than a year old, and comments that he may now depart in peace.

Anna is also there. She is a prophetess who, we are told, hasn't left the temple in eighty-four years after the death of her husband. She is an intercessor. Both she and Simeon have given their lives to praying for the consolation of Israel.

Anna is thought to be around one hundred and five years old. Can you imagine a life spent waiting and waiting? The faithfulness of her prayers overwhelms me. Such patience and endurance. I imagine them, like the image in the book of Revelation, being stored up in a bowl in heaven to be poured out over the earth.

Each of their stories does little work to advance the overall gospel account of Christ. They are almost asides. It's not surprising that they aren't included in the other Gospels. They might even seem inconsequential . . . to spend your life simply waiting for Jesus.

And yet their appearance here is like God's tip of the hat to something he loves and that we might otherwise miss. Similar to the story of the widow's mite, we are being shown something small, and yet of deep value in God's kingdom. God finds stories of patient waiting deeply inspiring.

Simeon speaks words of profound insight. He recognizes two things that stand out to me. First, the work of redemption isn't just for Israel, but for all the world. Second, this radical inclusivity will bring with it suffering and rejection. For Jesus, and also for Mary. He says, "This child is destined to cause the falling and rising of many in Israel, and to be a sign that will be spoken against, so that the thoughts of many hearts will be revealed. And a sword will pierce your own soul too" (Luke 2:34-35).

I imagine this isn't what Mary was hoping to hear. It makes me think of that scene in the movie *The Passion of the Christ* where Jesus, carrying his cross, turns to his mother and says, "See, Mother, I make all things new." Such tenderness and humanity!

Simeon was able to see that consolation and suffering are inextricably linked. That hearts that love like Jesus must both widen and deepen. In order to rise, we must fall.

The wisdom of Simeon was forged in the waiting. Here is a man who spent his whole life patiently staring into God's masterpiece. And what comes forth from his heart is perspective that left them all in awe. He understood the heart of the true artist. He understood the deeper work God was doing. He trusted the slow work of God.

The middle place is not a destination to arrive at or a place to visit and leave. Instead, it is a way of being. A way of loving. A way of engaging. Ultimately, it is the way of Jesus.

There is a place I go to intentionally to slow down. It is an abbey in the high desert called St. Andrew's. It's a place I go to listen, to draw alongside the silence of stone. The quiet there can be felt. Its calmness claims me.

I love this abbey because of its depth and simplicity. It is modest and unpretentious, almost stark. It mimics its context of high desert. Cold and almost barren, and yet bursting forth with life.

When I go to St. Andrew's Abbey, I am confronted everywhere by
the crucifix. It is there, always present—the suffering savior. At the
abbey, you are always in the gaze of the suffering Christ. The invitation is to meet eyes with Jesus in the place of his suffering. To see
past your own sins that put him there and to receive the grace being
offered. It is convicting. It is painful. And it is ultimately freeing.

My friend Steve leads an exercise where you prayerfully imagine
yourself standing at the foot of the cross. It lasts nine minutes, the
length of two songs he plays in the background. As you stand or
kneel, he encourages you to slowly bring your gaze from the pierced
feet of Jesus, past his garments and brokenness, to look deeply into
the eyes of the Savior.

Having participated in this exercise several times over the years,
I am always in awe of how much emotion is released in the partici-
pants, and in my own heart as well. Always there are many tears.
Tears of sorrow and joy. Tears of penitence and gratitude. Sometimes
there is resistance and frustration. Once a student even got angry at
Steve for making her experience the depth of that pain.

Martin Luther said, in his Easter Book, "If one does meditate
rightly on the suffering of Christ for a day, an hour, or even a quarter
of an hour, this we may confidently say is better than a whole year
of fasting, days of Psalm singing, yes, than even one hundred Masses,
because this reflection changes the whole man/woman and makes
them new, as once they were in baptism."

The cross is the middle place, and there Christ continues to
remain in that place of sacrificial love, beckoning us to join him
there. I realize that my evangelical tradition has often rushed to the
empty tomb. Like skipping to the end of the story. The happy ending
without the deep cost. Cheap grace, as Bonhoeffer describes it.

So often I settle for cheap grace myself, if I'm honest. I still prefer
the accolades of getting good grades to the grit and discipline required to really learn life's lessons. I want to see immediate fruit

instead of patiently allowing the seeds to take root and the fruit to come in its proper time and season.

To trust in the slow work of God can be incredibly freeing. When my agenda or my dysfunctional ways of measuring value are laid aside, I can rest in the work that God is doing and I begin to see the depth of beauty that only God can create. But the grace that this extends to me pertains not only to ourselves alone. It is how God sees everyone. As works in progress. As unfinished paintings. How hurriedly we pass over the work God is doing because we fail to see the depth or we are too distracted by our own appearances.

Part of the freedom that comes with waiting is the dawning realization that those around me are suffering under the same burdens of insecurity and self-scrutiny. To stop obsessing over my own blemishes allows me to look past the blemishes of others. Or to not merely overlook them, but see through them to the depths of the broken beauty of redemption. The deepest work of God happens in the furnace of suffering. And the outcome isn't just pleasing to the eye. It is heavy and refined and pure.

Once again, the gift of suffering yields both glory and self-forgetfulness. But the fruit is in so much more than the celebration of God's work in my own heart. It's in the joy of seeing and marveling over that work in others. It's in seeing the beauty of each piece of art, and the brilliance of the artist behind each work.

And above all, it's in savoring the most profound piece of artistry —Christ crucified. This depiction of the ultimate gift, this sacrificial love at its most pure. Courage and vulnerability at its most raw. And in the brokenness of his body and the pouring out of his blood, we see God's heart laid bare.

Our lives must necessarily follow this same path. We too must be broken, before we can be renewed. We must endure before we can be transformed. And we must yield our hearts for them to grow. Teresa of Ávila said, in *The Interior Castle*, "Fix your eyes on the Crucified and everything will become small for you." And this is true. The self becomes small. But it also comes alive.

FOR REFLECTION AND CONVERSATION

1. How do you relate to the image of the unfinished painting? Do you ever find yourself wanting to hurry the process?

2. Do you ever wish truth felt simpler or more concise? How comfortable are you with mystery? How is the slow work of God requiring you to patiently accept God's timeline instead of your own?

3. Have you, like Simeon and Anna, found yourself waiting and waiting for an unanswered promise of God? How does this feel to wait so long? What questions does waiting raise about who God is?

4. How does the suffering of Christ on the cross speak into our times of waiting? How does Christ model long-suffering for us in a way that we can follow? How does it put our suffering into perspective?

PART 4

THE WAY OF THE RIVER

TRANSFORMATION CAN FEEL IMPOSSIBLE TO MEASURE. There simply isn't an adequate metric. We measure growth by creating a system that we can quantify, by creating a way to attempt to count it. But the transformation of our heart is much more subtle and nuanced. We are being slowly shaped from within. And as we are carried by this flow of change, we can lose vision. Especially when it feels like we're still struggling with the same old thing. Like we're just going around the circle one more time.

Seasons are like this. Time is like this. The seasons start to blur amid the redundancy. And pretty soon we can lose sight of where we've been and where we're going. It feels like we're never going to change. Like we might as well just accept that this is as far as we go.

But the truth is, we do change. And while we may not receive a ceremony or certificate when our hearts are enlarged, we must do our best to pay attention to the growth. Because without vision, our hearts perish. But also, as our hearts grow, so does our ability to see and respond with deep gratitude.

In C. S. Lewis's *Prince Caspian*, Lucy sees the lion, Aslan, after several years of being away, and exclaims that he has grown. The lion smiles back and corrects her: it is actually she who has grown.

When I think of spiritual transformation, I think we need to move away from our image of the wavy line into something more three dimensional. Our growth isn't mere further progression, but an act of becoming larger. Our growth isn't so compartmentalized, but instead is more holistic. Like the rings of a tree. We are expanding. Our

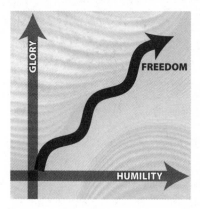

capacity for love and joy and generosity increases all at once. We aren't just improving, we are becoming something new.

The measurement isn't seen in how we look or feel, but in how we see. The lens through which we see the tensions of life. The way we look at relationships. And most importantly, how we see God.

13

LIVING IN JOY
AND GRIEF

THIS HAS BEEN A HEAVY WEEK. Two young men from Laguna died this week, separately. I still don't have all the details.

One of them I didn't know at all, but I spent some time this week with his family. This is one of the hardest assignments of being a pastor, to walk into that space of deep grief, to attempt to bring some comfort to unfamiliar faces in the place of despair. I feel so inadequate, and yet it is a role that I deeply value.

The other boy who died, I knew well. He was previously a student in my youth ministry. In fact, I've had a card from him sitting on my desk that I received a year ago. It contains sweet words of his growth and gratitude that reveal the rich depth of his heart.

It happens from time to time, where the darkness seems to be winning. When the clouds get so thick and heavy that it completely blocks out the sun. It can be overwhelming and, if you let it, defeating.

He wrote in his card, "Your words and grace have influenced me for the better. You have given me a gift and I took it. After receiving it, I have felt inspired."

Rereading his words brings both comfort and an ache. My mind is filled with memories and clips of tender moments with him. I know he's in a better place.

And yet this week has not been without glimmers of joy and beauty.

I paddled out with dear friends last night, surfing in warm water and enjoying that beautiful calm at the end of the day. I love those times of meaningful conversation while floating, interrupted briefly by the set waves and then the paddle back out. Afterward we sat in their backyard, playing ping-pong, throwing bags, and savoring summer. I felt so lucky.

Somehow, life seems to hold out both goodness and grief all at once. It can be a bit disorienting. To experience pleasure in the midst of grief can cause guilt and even accusing feelings of betrayal. But what I am slowly realizing is that the two emotions of joy and grief speak into each other. Our pain gives context to the beauty, and the beauty gives meaning to the pain. It is mysterious, and, at times, feels more than we can bear. But the beauty assures us that there is a deep "okayness" beyond this world, to paraphrase Richard Rohr from his daily devotions. And so we cling to the good. We follow it all the way to its source. And there, we are reminded that the sun is still shining beyond the clouds.

Grief reminds us just how costly it is to love. It is what we risk when we vulnerably expose our hearts. And heartache is unavoidably intertwined with intimacy. In a way, it signifies that we are living well. David Whyte says this about heartbreak in *Consolations*:

> Heartbreak is not a visitation but a path that human beings follow through even the most average life. Heartbreak is an indication of our sincerity. Heartbreak is the beautifully helpless side of love and affection and is just as much an essence and emblem of care as the spiritual athlete's quick but abstract ability to let go.

Heartbreak is the inevitable fruit of living courageous lives. It merits the cost, because the joy we experience in selflessly loving another is worth the pain we experience in their loss. Because joy is what gives life its rich texture. These moments of connection pull us into the present. They fill our lives with depth and meaning. They fill our hearts with gratitude.

I often see this when sitting with people in spiritual direction. Usually we'll be discussing a matter that is heavy on their hearts or something they are wrestling with. Most people start going to direction when faced with a wilderness in their lives and come seeking a companion to journey with them. As we explore their wilderness together, sometimes the conversation will have run its course or ended up in a sort of cul-de-sac. We get stuck in the pain or the despair that comes from not seeing a way out. In these moments, I'll often ask if they've experienced any glimpses of consolation from God elsewhere in their lives. Have there been any surprises of joy or experiences of God's presence that have occurred outside of their field of vision? And nine times out of ten there have been. The glimpses can feel separate or disconnected. The look I often get at first is, 'What does this have to do with what we're talking about?'

But I believe these moments of joy are intimately connected with grief. The two form and inform each other. The grief gives our lives depth and meaning, while the joy provides us with the necessary hope and strength. To fail to see their connection leaves us at a disadvantage and, if we aren't careful, can pull us into a downward spiral. Seeing God's invitation in the glimpses of joy does work. It takes the despair and reframes it.

Reframing is a word that is showing up more and more these days, especially in the world of tech innovation. It is defined by *Mosby's Pocket Dictionary of Medicine, Nursing & Health Professions* as "changing the conceptual and/or emotional viewpoint in relation to which a situation is experienced and placing it in a different frame that fits the 'facts' of a concrete situation equally well, thereby changing its entire meaning."

In their book *Designing Your Life*, Stanford professors Bill Burnett and Dave Evans take principles from design and innovation and apply them to the question of "Who do I want to be when I grow up?" Or more accurately, "What do I want to grow into?" It reads like a couple of tech entrepreneurs doing spiritual formation, or at least life coaching.

One of the concepts they stress early in the book is the necessity of reframing. According to Burnett and Evans, this is how designers get unstuck—how they know they are working on the right problem. "Life design involves key reframes that allow you to step back, examine your biases, and open up new solution spaces."

Reframing is a way of seeing differently, of getting ourselves to look at our circumstances from a different viewpoint. And if we're honest, this can be almost impossible for us without some serious and intentional effort.

I'm reminded of David Foster Wallace's joke at the beginning of his commencement address at Kenyon, where he talks about the older fish swimming past two younger fish and asking, "Hey boys, how's the water?" and the two younger fish looking puzzled and one saying, "What's water?" Without reframing, context becomes meaningless.

Reframing requires us to detach from our emotions, from our thoughts, from our bodies, from our context, settings, and circumstances. If we don't detach, our thoughts and feelings can own us. They control us. And if you're like me, my thoughts and feelings can feed off each other. They fuel each other. If I'm feeling anxious, I start pulling it apart in my mind, thinking through worst-case scenarios, anticipating what else might go wrong. And these thoughts just spiral back into more emotional fuel, more worry, more anxiety, and so I begin to unpack those feelings in my mind . . . on and on. It is the downward spiral of impending doom.

Reframing allows us to simply observe our thoughts and emotions. To name them. To treat them gently and without judgment.

But also to observe them as if from the side of the road, and not standing in the middle of traffic.

And when I do this, I am embarrassed to admit, I am often surprised to find God right by my side. Near me. Present in the midst of whatever emotional or circumstantial storm has been swirling around me. And I realize that God has been there all along. Patiently waiting.

My church has been studying the psalms, and it has been fun to watch how David uses these prayerful songs to reframe his circumstances. Whether surrounded by enemies, hiding in a cave, fleeing from his palace, or alone in the wilderness, he prays. And as he does, his context changes. His life is reframed. He is able to notice the water and even swim against it instead of being helplessly swept along by it.

One of my favorite moments in David's story is when he is fleeing from Saul with his band of mighty men. He reminds me of a Robin Hood or William Wallace, fighting for his people and for God while hiding for his life. One of the places David finds solace is in the caves of En Gedi. They become a refuge for him and one of the places in which he finds safety from his enemies.

David is wrongfully accused and is living in such hardship. There is no comfort of food and warmth of a home. He is in a place of deep loneliness and despair, and from this place writes some of his most beautiful psalms.

The psalms teach us how to pray, and David holds nothing back. His emotion is strong and unedited. His enemies are real and are constantly lurking around him and setting traps for him. As David prays we feel his brokenness, his anger, and his feelings of desolation.

But as he prays, we begin to watch his world transform. The cave becomes not merely a hiding place, but a sanctuary. In the midst of his prayer, the reality of God's nearness is revealed. Instead of being removed from his circumstances, they are recontextualized. The world gets larger. David's vision transcends the limits of his hiding place, and he finds himself instead in the shadow of God's wings.

Reframing our lives in this way helps us to both spot dysfunctional beliefs that have crept in and realign our circumstances with the awareness of God's provisions of grace and steadfast love. And this allows us to transcend. To go above. To see our lives and ourselves, not only with a greater sense of awareness, but with the stabilizing promise that all things work together for good. Even when our thoughts, emotions, and circumstances are swirling about us like a tempest, God is near.

The climax of the cave story happens when Saul, David's accuser and enemy, walks directly into the cave David is hiding in with several of his men. Saul is there to relieve himself, which puts him at quite a disadvantage. It is an opportunity, a gift. David's men tell him as much. God has delivered to David his enemy. All it would take is one quick stroke of the sword and they could return to Jerusalem, with all the comforts of the palace. God has given them a quick way out of the cave.

But David doesn't fall for it. This isn't a gift; it is a test. So David instead sneaks up and cuts off a piece of Saul's robe. It is an awkward moment. Either David was extremely stealthy, or Saul was concentrating really hard. Maybe it was both.

The point is that David was wise enough not to take matters into his own hands. He demonstrates such wisdom. David comes out of the cave to confront Saul with the reality that he has spared his life. He affirms that he will continue to yield to Saul's authority as king and not take the crown for himself. It is one of David's best moments. He holds his preordained kingship with open hands. And by doing it, protects his heart from becoming like Saul's.

This is the power of reframing: it exposes us to a higher level of wisdom. It allows us to transcend our circumstances to a place of deeper wisdom. It reminds me of Einstein's quote that no problem can be solved from the same level of consciousness that created it. Without leaving the cave, we must get beyond it.

Because to take the crown by force would only replace Saul with another Saul. In an act of deep restraint, David chooses to remain in the wilderness and not shortcut the deeper work that God is doing in his own heart. It is a brilliant act of faith. But it is not blind. Instead, it is informed by God's presence and comfort in the cave. God's presence doesn't remove David from his trials and circumstances, but instead lifts his eyes to see a much greater vision for his life.

In *The Tale of Three Kings*, Gene Edwards writes, "[David] seemed to grasp a deep understanding of the unfolding drama in which he had been caught. He seemed to understand something that few of even the wisest men of his day understood. . . . God wanted a broken vessel."

This is one of the counterintuitive but signature acts of God. The way up is the way down. Transcendence requires meekness and humility. Our strength is demonstrated best in surrender.

An excerpt from the brilliant Puritan prayer called "The Valley of Vision," says,

Let me learn that to have nothing is to possess all,
Let me learn that to bear the cross is to wear the crown,
Let me learn that to give is to receive,
that the valley is the place of vision.

Without this vision, our lives ultimately fall into indulgence. God's work becomes merely self-improvement, disconnected from God's intention of sacrificial love. Our growth is not primarily for ourselves but for others. Without suffering, our hearts are turned inward toward self and our world begins to shrink.

✧ ◆ ✧

Another beautiful story of reframing in Scripture happens when Paul and Silas are wrongfully imprisoned. Sitting in this place of injustice, the two begin to sing. Their voices lift them beyond their imprisonment. Their hearts soar freely.

And then an earthquake occurs. It shakes the prisoners free. Their bonds are loosed. And if I were Paul, I would have said a quick "Thank you, Lord" and fled. Why else would God collapse the prison? This is a sign of God's love for Paul, that he comes in and rescues him. But that isn't what Paul does. Instead, he remains. The earthquake isn't a gift of provision, but instead a test. Paul remains and convinces the other prisoners to do the same. Because the jailer of the prison will be executed if Paul escapes. And this story isn't about Paul. It is about the jailer.

When the jailer sees Paul's profound integrity and submission to God, he is moved to the point of repentance and surrenders himself. His life is redeemed. Paul's self-restraint along with deep trust yields eternal fruit.

The economy of God's kingdom operates on a much different currency than our own. Faith takes deep work. It costs us our comfort. It pushes us toward our vulnerability. It requires us to look honestly into our hearts and to see our fragility and weakness. This requires an enormous amount of trust.

Which is why these glimpses of his grace are so crucial for our growth. Without these windows into God's heart, the suffering and despair overwhelm us. The heartbreak becomes too much. We disconnect instead of remaining. But to grab hold of these moments creates hope. The kindness of God renews our strength. The joy allows us to remain. And as we do, we transcend.

Sometimes the winter months get so long and hard, we stop looking for the signs of spring. We get so focused on surviving the frost that we fail to see the blossoms as they start to bloom. We don't recognize the subtle chirping of the birds outside as the beginning of a new season.

As I think of the loss of these two young men this week, my heart breaks, for them and for their families. Their winter has just begun. There are no simple answers that will bring a quick remedy. These wounds will never completely heal.

But when Christ enters the picture, my heart is able to be at peace. When I can hold on to moments of joy, my heart is able to be at rest, not needing to fix or minimize to bring about an artificial comfort. The joy becomes my strength. And it points me back to the heart of my God. A God who sees and feels, who suffers and grieves, and who also savors the goodness that life brings.

It is in times like these that gratitude becomes one of our dearest friends. Gratitude helps us relish life's goodness without diminishing the suffering. It allows us to celebrate friendship without mourning what has been lost. The joy and pleasure of friendship, when seen as the true gift it is, is often enough to keep us present not only through our suffering, but also through that of others.

In spiritual direction, I'll often ask the question, "Where is God in this?" Because the truth is, God is usually right there. And we've somehow lost sight of him in our grief. In the cave. At the hospital bedside. The question reminds us that he is closer than we thought, but not where we were necessarily looking or expecting him to be. Seeing God requires us to not just turn our head, but to take a step back. To widen our gaze. And when we do, we see that we're not alone. That God's answer, though indirect, is there. And it is enough.

The joy may merely be the first little glimpse of new life sprouting up. Fruit may still be a long way off. But those leaves mean so much more than a simple shift of seasons. They are hope. And hope reframes everything.

FOR REFLECTION AND CONVERSATION

1. Have you experienced times of simultaneous joy and grief? Can you see a connection between the two?

2. Have you experienced grief that led you to a place of despair? Were you able to find God in the midst of your suffering? How does God's presence reframe your sorrow? How does God's presence affect one's perspective?

3. Maybe you find yourself grieving today. Have you lost your hope? How has God answered these moments in your past? How might God be giving you a glimmer of hope today?

14

THE TENSION
OF GLORY
AND HUMILITY

I'VE ALWAYS LOVED THE OUTDOORS. I love to surf and backpack
and rock climb. It has always been the place where I feel most like
myself. In the ocean, my soul is refreshed. In the mountains, my heart
becomes calm. And on the side of the cliff, everything comes alive.

I remember a time when a huge swell was hitting and I met my
friend before sunrise at Trestles, a popular surf spot in San Clemente.
Trestles has a long walk down and I remember you could hear the
booming of the surf all the way up at the parking lot almost a mile
away. Trestles is a bit like Disneyland—an amazing wave and always
crowded. That day I was nervous just paddling out. On every wave
there were four or five guys that would take off. It was a circus.
Leashes snapping, boards breaking . . . it was chaos. I remember a
large set coming in and paddling over each wave and watching everyone dropping in on each other. And then there was one more and,
at that point, I was the only one, sitting by myself. Everyone had
gone on the earlier waves and so I swung around, alone, on a wave
that was clearly meant for me.

I can still picture it as I dropped in. The sun was just up and the
whole wave lit up at once, this long beautiful line, and as I bottom
turned the whole lineup raised their arms. It was glorious. I rode

the wave all the way to the beach and as I started paddling back out my friend was inside. He looked at me and said, "Did you see that?!" I was thinking, *See that? I was that.* He said, "As you were dropping in two dolphins jumped out of the face of the wave behind you." I remember being like, "Oh, yeah, of course I saw that. Who didn't see that?"

Ah, humility . . . and glory. Somehow, right there is where I'm at my best. Veer to either extreme and I'm the worst version of myself—either insecure or egotistical. But in that center, held in tension, that is my true self. That is what I'm being called to.

And as silly as that story may be, I think it demonstrates God's heart. He celebrates the joy that comes as I slide to my feet, the rush of spray flying up the face of the wave, and the stomach churning feeling of a large drop. He takes pleasure in my pleasure as I savor the feelings of speed and the beauty of a wave face opening up to the morning sunlight. It is gorgeous and glorious.

But as my mind turns toward those around me, that small, wretched side of myself wants even more than it deserves. It wants more than joy. It wants adoration. It lives on an unhealthy diet of accolades. And that is where God, mercifully, cuts me off and reminds me that I'm really not that big of a deal.

But it takes courage to live in this vulnerable tension. It isn't safe. It demands more of me than I want to give. It pushes me further than I want to go toward glory and also diminishes me where I'd prefer to be seen. I resist it, and yet my heart longs for it. Because self-forgetful joy is one of the greatest gifts in life. It is freedom.

I've been backpacking my whole life and had the opportunity a few years ago to take my son with me for the first time. It was such a gift passing on to him something so meaningful to me, and he asked as we were hiking what it was I liked so much about hiking in the backcountry. I think he asked it somewhere in the grueling first five miles of uphill and he was trying to figure what I could possibly be enjoying about it. I told him that when I'm immersed in creation, when I've left behind all the comforts and distractions of normal life, it is there I most clearly hear the voice of God. That was interesting to him, and also to me. It wasn't what I was expecting to say. He asked me why that was the case, and I think I've been unpacking that question ever since.

Augustine and others referred to creation as the book of nature. It long preceded the written word. It was primarily from the book of nature that we first understood the presence and character of God. Through the lens of nature, we see beyond our world into something bigger.

And creation is sometimes referred to as God's first language. The beauty and design and creativity reveal God's heart and mind. Scripture itself tells us that God's power and attributes can be seen in creation. In fact, all of humanity is held accountable to this reality. We are expected to not only notice the beauty of creation, but to see through it, as a lens, to the character and heart of God.

As I reflect on the idea of hearing God's voice in nature, I think the first reason for this is that it gets me out of my head. As I've said, I'm a pretty cerebral guy, and an introvert. I like to take my ideas and emotions to my "mind palace." I like figuring out the puzzles. But the problem is, when I'm listening for God's voice indoors, it sounds an awful lot like my own. And this can be dangerous.

Because I can rationalize just about anything. Without knowing it, I take the premise that I would prefer and reverse engineer a logical defense. And then I convince myself I deduced the whole thing, and not the other way around.

I've heard it said that when we worship, we are often worshiping a flattering image of ourselves. I definitely see this tendency in me.

I love comfort over conflict; I prefer affirmation to correction. I love compliments over critique. But, as a result, when I mistake my voice for God's, he has a tendency to tell me I'm doing a pretty great job and to just keep doing what I'm doing.

I like how Anne Lamott's priest friend told her, "You can safely assume you've created God in your own image when it turns out that God hates all the same people you do."

What I appreciate about nature is that it resists my self-rationalizations. It has an unchangeable reality to it that isn't up for negotiation. And sometimes it has to remind us of this fact, often painfully. I remember shattering my ankle rock climbing and realizing that I'm not immortal. I'm breakable. Dallas Willard says reality is what we bump into when we're wrong.

This isn't a virtual, online, videogame world. Reality isn't simply what we make it or desire it to be. All it takes is one weird pain in our bodies to realize that we aren't in control. And conforming our lives to this greater reality is critical to navigating through life.

For example, I was driving in the Whole Foods parking lot the other night when an older woman stepped out in front of my car. I slammed on the brakes and just avoided hitting her. She didn't even look up—she was staring at her phone. I thought, *What is she doing? Taking a picture?* And then I saw her start flicking the screen and realized she was catching a Pokémon. That poor woman almost got a taste of actual reality crashing into her virtual world!

Years ago I went with a friend to the E3 convention, which is all about tech and games. There was a banner for Mountain Dew that said, "We understand that killing the dragon and rescuing the princess is more important than your day job." That's hilarious, but also really disturbing.

The problem with self-rationalization is that we create our own realities and stories for ourselves that are much too small. We choose a virtual life that is comfortable and safe. And, as it turns out, boring. Underneath it all, we long for something bigger, deeper, and more meaningful.

Our cities put off so much light that we can barely see the stars at night. The stars disappear until we move far enough away from this ceiling of artificial light. And then, what we see is majestic. We realize our proper place in the universe. What I love about going outdoors is that the world gets bigger and I get smaller. It is humbling.

One night I watched a documentary on the Hubble telescope. Back in 1995 the leader of the program was able to point the Hubble anywhere he liked for ten days. He pointed it at the very darkest place they found in the night sky. For ten days they took pictures. They came away with an image called the Hubble Ultra-Deep Field.

That light has traveled over 13 billion light years to get to us. It is over three times as old as the earth. Each dot is a galaxy, which means billions of stars. The cosmos is beautiful, it is vast, and it is dangerous. There are galaxies there that are actually eating other galaxies. As David writes in Psalm 8,

> When I consider your heavens,
> the work of your fingers,
> the moon and the stars,
> which you have set in place,
> what is mankind that you are mindful of them,
> human beings that you care for them?

That is the God we pray to. My egocentric little world collapses at that image. I realize I'm not that important. That life is not about me.

Scripture tells us that this is the necessary place from which we can listen and hear. It is fear of the Lord. It is humbling. And it is where wisdom begins. It makes us silent. What are human beings? But the psalmist goes on. He writes,

But you have made them a little lower than the angels
    and crowned them with glory and honor.

Somehow this too is true. It is paradoxical. Humanity is both majestic and insignificant. We live in the place of both glory and humility. It is a necessary tension.

I read a physicist recently who said that the principle of comple-
mentarity in physics tells us that we can know a deep truth when its
opposite is also a deep truth. If that is true, then this is one of the deep
ones. We are both great and small. And God wants us to pursue both!

We tend to prefer a sort of middle ground. To be spiritually middle
class instead of being both rich and poor. But the fact is, God is
pulling us in opposite directions at once. G. K. Chesterton says in
Orthodoxy, "Christianity got over the difficulty of combining furious
opposites, by keeping them both, and keeping them both furious."
God furiously wants both our glory and our meekness.

There's a story that I love by William Faulkner called "The Bear."
It's from his book *Go Down Moses*. The main character, a boy named
Ike McCaslin, is ten and has been invited to join the men on the fall
hunting trip into the deep woods. The ultimate goal is a bear that
they've named Old Ben. Ben is this legendary bear that roams an area
of one hundred square miles and torments farmers by carrying off
their livestock. Even young calves. The hunting dogs fear him,
bullets don't seem to harm him. Ike is both frightened and fasci-
nated by the stories he hears.

He meets a man named Sam Fathers who takes him under his
wing. Sam teaches him the necessary patience and humility required
to hunt. One night they hear the dogs barking this high pitched bark
of fear and Sam tells Ike that's Ben. He's come to check out the
hunters. He does it every year.

Ike begins to learn to track and one evening, all of sudden, the forest goes quiet. Ike can feel this presence but he can't see or hear anything. And then the moment passes and the sound returns. He asks Sam about it and Sam tells him that was Old Ben. Ike says, "I couldn't see him," and Sam replies that it was Ben that was doing the looking.

Ike realizes that he has a choice to make. He wants so badly to see the bear. But the fact that he is carrying a gun prevents this. And so he leaves his gun behind. He continues to learn to track until he starts finding Ben's footprints, following him deeper and deeper into the forest. He reaches the edge of the deepest woods, where he's never been, and realizes that it is not enough to leave behind his weapon. He sets down his walking stick and his compass, and enters into the unknown.

Eventually he comes to this enormous footprint that is half filled with water and realizes that he is close. He enters into an open space, a deep glade. And there he sees the bear. As Faulkner writes, "It did not emerge, appear; it was just there, immobile, fixed in the green and windless noon's hot dappling, not as big as he had dreamed it but big as he had expected, bigger, dimensionless against the dappled obscurity, looking at him." The animal moves across the glade, pauses briefly, and then passes into the obscurity of the woods.

Jeremiah 29:13 says, "You will seek me and find me when you seek me with all your heart." All our heart requires courage. That is what courage actually means. To expose your heart, to make it vulnerable. This is where our eyes are opened to the greater spiritual realities surrounding us. When we see from this place of humility, courage, and vulnerability, we are seeing with the heart, or what Scripture refers to as the eyes of the heart.

In the story of "The Bear," for Ike to see Old Ben, he must be disarmed. He must lay aside the things that give him an advantage or that produce a sense of control and comfort. He comes to the bear on the bear's terms. And at each stage there is a choice, and with it, the temptation to turn back.

Our spiritual growth requires of us the very same thing. To see God, we must be willing to be seen. We must lay aside our false securities, and we must embrace the terrifying and yet freeing light of truth. For most of us, it can feel like more than we can endure. We'd prefer to hide indoors.

But it is in the outdoors where my eyes are opened to the reality that God is all around me. Jacob makes this statement when he awakes from a dream: "Surely the LORD is in this place, and I was not aware of it" (Genesis 28:16). When I go outdoors I am faced with truth, with goodness and glory, and with beauty. These things draw my heart toward the realities of both who I am and who God is. And my heart is awakened.

There is a story Eugene Peterson tells in his introduction to Wangerin's book *Whole Prayer*, about John Muir visiting a friend in the Sierras who had recently built a cabin. His friend invited him to visit right at the moment that a huge storm was hitting. His friend told him this is why he had built this place, a place of comfort and security in the midst of the storm. And then he realized that John was putting on his raincoat. "Where are you going?" John Muir said, "I don't want to miss this." He climbed to the top of the ridge and climbed the tallest tree and experienced the fullness and wildness of the storm.

There is a choice in all this, at least to a point—to live a life in the safety of the indoors where we create a small world of comfort and security. But, if we're honest, this story isn't just boring to others. We bore ourselves. It is too small. You are made for so much more.

When I go outdoors, this small self withers away. I am confronted with a reality that is greater than myself. And I begin to immerse myself in it. It speaks to my very center and draws it out.

Being outdoors is sacramental. It is immersive and experiential. The lessons it teaches transcend our spiritual language. The outdoors is the wildlands of our transformative journey. It is the desert of the unknown, both literally and metaphorically. It is the place where we are tested and where we grow. But it is also the place where we come alive. Where we discover the reason for all the work we've been doing. Where meaning isn't found in simple goals and easy answers. Where God doesn't fit in our nice and convenient boxes. Where our deepest fears are conquered and overcome. Where the limits of our belief, discovered in our anxiety, are seen and moved beyond. Where our God beckons us to come deeper and further in. And we feel so small and inadequate. And at the same time, like we've finally found a story big enough to capture our hearts.

FOR REFLECTION AND CONVERSATION

1. Do you identify with the tendency to embellish stories or to rationalize away feelings of guilt? Have you experienced moments of truth that left you feeling embarrassed or exposed? Do you find yourself preferring your version of the story to the truth itself?

2. In the story of the bear, Ike is disarmed before he is able to see. He lays aside the things that give him a sense of control. How is God disarming you? What are you being asked to lay aside? What in your life keeps you from truly seeking and finding?

3. The outdoors are wild. They humble us. Yet they are also the place of wild adventure. Where is God leading you out from? What is God leading you toward?

15

THE WISDOM
OF THE RIVER

O NE OF MY DEAREST MEMORIES with my kids happened in a
river. We were in Big Sky, Montana, with my parents, and making
day trips into Yellowstone. But halfway through the trip, I stole away
with my two oldest children and hired a fly-fishing guide to take us
out for a couple of hours on the Gallatin River. It was magical.

I grew up fishing—in lakes on family trips to Minnesota as a kid,
off the pier for halibut with my grandpa, catching rainbow trout in
the Sierras on backpacking trips . . . but always with bait. Never with
flies. And I guess I always felt like I was missing out on something.
Fly-fishing is where the true mastery lies. It is artistic, and it is contemplative. And it appealed to the purist in me.

We put on our waders and stepped carefully into the rushing river.
It was like stepping right into the set of *A River Runs Through It*.
Gorgeous colors, an enormous cliff backdrop, and a dark, winding,
roping river that we were soon up to our waists in.

Our guide was brilliant. He had graduated from an Ivy League
school, but opted to live the life of a guide, skiing in winters and
fishing all summer. He set each of us up with our poles, tied our flies
on, and then showed us not only how to cast, but where. "You see
that hole right there? Just put it right there and you'll get a bite."

I remember asking, "How do you know there are fish in that spot
right there? Can you see them?"

He replied, "I don't need to see them. They *have* to be there. That's how the river works."

Now I still don't fully understand what he meant by that, but sure enough, a couple casts later and I had a bite. What a wonderful moment when your rod bends deep and you feel the powerful pull of the fish. It fought hard, but eventually we landed him. A beautiful trout, the biggest fish I'd ever caught.

A few moments later my son landed an even bigger one. What joy it is to watch and experience his delight. I sure love that kid. Sometimes it hurts how much.

After that I hooked another one. An even bigger fish this time, but I couldn't quite land him. I reeled him in all the way to my feet when he suddenly wiggled free, spit out the fly, and splashed away from me, laughing to himself, I'm sure. It was then, in my helplessness, that I realized that our guide had moved further down the river, out of my line of sight. He had moved on because Gabe and I already had our fish. He was entirely focused on my daughter, Mia.

I knew our time was coming to an end, so Gabe and I (and Patty, who was snapping photos) all walked down to see how Mia was doing. What a gorgeous view as we rounded the bend. There was my daughter standing out there in the middle of the stream, fishing with such grace. She has this beautiful, flawless cast. Gabe's cast was good, mine was kind of forced, but Mia's just flowed. She was a natural.

I asked the guide how it was going, and he said she'd had bite after bite, but that she couldn't quite set the hook. I could see that look of determination in her eyes—the one where she is doing everything in her power to will back the tears.

And then, as the last seconds of our time were melting away, as the beautifully cast line hit the water, bam! Her pole bent to what looked like the breaking point. As her little hands reeled in the fish, I could see our guide immediately at her side. He wasn't going to let this one get away. (I'm sure experience told him his tip increased exponentially when he could get a 100 percent success rate.)

She landed that fish and I remember breathing a huge sigh of relief. What heartache it would have been for her to be the only one who didn't get a fish. Especially for my middle child. My little perfectionist. My daughter, who gets report cards with straight A+s. So much pressure!

There was such a simple joy in that moment. As we trudged back in our soaking waders, I remember trying so hard to embed the memory deep in my mind. I didn't want to lose this. So much of life is a constant struggle to remain present. It feels like chipping away at something that we can't quite see in its entirety. And then, every once in a while we get these profound moments of deep joy.

We get just a glimpse. A peek past the curtain. And the goodness is almost too good to be true. The simple beauty envelops us. And all there is to do is sit back and absorb it.

There is something so enrapturing about a river. When camping, I always want to get that spot as close as possible to the water's edge (without breaking the rules of course). Rivers are wonderful to look at, to wade in, to fish out of, to swim in, but more than anything, to listen to. There is such a lyrical elegance to a flowing stream.

It reminds me of a line from Wendell Berry's poem "The Real Work." He writes, "The impeded stream is the one that sings." Maybe this is part of the mystique of rivers. They have such power and strength, and yet yield and bend. And as the waters rush over and around the rock and various impediments, it bursts into song.

Throughout Scripture, the river is the image of the divine life and flow of God. Ezekiel is shown a vision of a river bursting forth from the temple and he is led into it at the hand of his guide, little by little, first his ankles, then knees, then up to his waist.

What a wonderful picture of our own spiritual journey, and the patience of our God to lead us deeper and deeper still. I've heard it said that God is easily pleased but not easily satisfied. The image of God standing further out and deeper than us in the water and beckoning us to join him is a welcoming image.

Psalm 46 tells us, "There is a river whose streams make glad the city of God." The stream refreshes us. It quenches our thirst. It washes us clean. It delights our hearts.

As my kids and I headed back from the river to our car, I was struck by the modest elegance of our fly-fishing experience. All of the goodness of life was felt in that simple moment. The beauty of nature, the artistry of the cast, the unpredictability of the catch, and the sweet connection with my children. My heart felt so full. Refreshed.

I wondered how much of our life we are chasing so hard after all the wrong things, hurrying past the quiet streams that beckon us to slow down, to take off our shoes, to wade in. So much of our problem is pace. We are always rushing. Always hurrying. Blaise Pascal writes in *Pensees*, "All of humanity's problems stem from man's inability to sit quietly in a room alone." I think he's right. Our hearts are terribly restless. They refuse to be still. To remain.

Psalm 46 tells us to "be still and know that I am God." The NASB translates "be still" instead as "cease striving." This is helpful. Because it isn't always enough to just pause. It isn't enough to stop moving. It is as if God is telling us to open up our clenched fist. To let go of the rope that we are clinging to. To fall back into his arms, even when we can't see. To stop trying to protect ourselves, to stop trying to control the future. To cease defending ourselves against the infinite number of dangers that could be lurking just around the corner. To be still can feel incredibly vulnerable.

The wisdom of the river runs counter to our human wisdom. In our world, results always require effort. Opportunities are earned. God helps those that help themselves. But the river beckons us instead to surrender. To yield. To allow it to carry us along.

I remember a time just before my senior year of high school when I desperately needed a summer job. I needed to save for college, to pay for insurance, and to be able to put gas in the VW bus I had inherited from my dad. I had agreed to get a job, though I knew it wasn't merely a suggestion. But so far, all my efforts were proving futile.

Around the same time, I had an opportunity to go with the junior high kids from my church as a counselor for summer camp up at Forest Home. I loved Forest Home, I loved camp, and I loved working with students. This was well before I became a youth pastor, or even knew it was a vocation I'd later step into. I just really wanted to go to camp with them.

I remember telling my dad that our church needed to know that afternoon if I could go and that I still didn't have a job for the summer. I was out of time. I asked him for leniency. "I'll start looking as soon as I get back from camp, I promise."

But my dad stood his ground. Not defiantly. I think he must have had some nudge or inkling that he wasn't supposed to bend on this one. Instead he said, "Have you prayed about it?" I told him I hadn't. He said, "Let's pray now." I remember thinking, *Dad, we've only got three hours. This isn't giving God enough time.*

As I think back on that moment, I realize that underlying that protest was fear, and with it, self-protection. It was such a risky fleece to put out there. I had no leads. I didn't even know where to begin. This was too big of an ask. And by asking, I was putting my heart out there in such a way that it could get broken.

I think sometimes we pray cautiously to protect our fragile faith. It makes sense. If our prayers go unanswered, then what does that mean? At the very least, it means that the simple desires of our hearts are uninteresting to God. Maybe he's even a little perturbed at my triviality. God has way bigger fish to fry.

Somewhat reluctantly, I humbly waded into the river of faith. "God, I need a job this summer, and I really want to counsel these kids at camp. If there is any way you could answer this within the next three hours, that would be great. Amen."

And then I sat and did nothing. There was nothing to do. I had no leads or options. I sat and waited, for an hour and a half . . . and then the phone rang. It was a man from my church whose name I recognized, but who I had never talked to before. He introduced himself and asked if I would be interested in working for him for the summer. I couldn't believe it. I spluttered that I would. He asked if I could start at the beginning of next week. I paused, and then I hesitatingly stammered, "I was hoping to counsel at camp next week." His response? "No problem. You can start the Monday you get back."

I looked at my watch. God still had an hour and a half to spare.

Moments like this give a statement like "cease striving" a little more teeth. I get the impression that God isn't just telling me what he is capable of doing, he is telling me how easy it is for him to do.

Because the provision is never the difficult part. We are. The difficulty lies in our hearts. Our hearts like to remain independent. Our hearts love control and security. But even more they like the anonymity and freedom of holding. At least mine does.

As a relational introvert, I enjoy being able to come and go as I please. Long emotional commitments overwhelm me. I'm always trying to be careful to manage my emotional fuel. Because when it is gone, I crash. It isn't a gradual decline. Instead, it is like the flame goes out. I'm out of gas.

I manage this energy by being careful of what I commit to. But life has this way of constantly asking too much of me. My role as pastor is one of constant emotional demands. So is my role as dad. And husband. As life progresses, the demands just seem to increase.

When my energy feels depleted, or when my schedule feels overcommitted beyond my reserves, I start to panic. I become afraid.

Afraid that I'll embarrass myself by saying the wrong thing, or I'll perform a wedding and I won't be able to set the right tone, or I'll preach and it will come out as confused or unprepared.

These are legitimate fears because each of these scenarios has happened multiple times. At least from my perspective. And the feeling is horrible. I feel naked and exposed. So much of my energy goes into keeping up appearances. So much so that it infiltrates my dreams.

I've had a reoccurring dream over the years, and in it, my teeth are falling out. It is like the roots are gone. My teeth have all become terribly loose and I can just reach in and pull them out without effort. After having this dream several times, I couldn't resist and googled what it meant. Several of the random websites I clicked said that the dream means you are worried that you are failing to keep up appearances.

I'm pretty sure that is right, because it is so convicting to me. How much of my emotional energy gets spent protecting my appearance? Looking the part, or presenting myself as strong. I spend so much time trying to avoid the embarrassing moments where my limitations are exposed, because then maybe people won't see me as having it all together. And that is where my power lies, right? In being impressive. Intelligent. Having it together.

That feels painful to write, because it is so obviously false. But that doesn't stop me from playing the game. I wonder if, really, the game is about fooling myself into thinking I am valuable, when, in fact, I truly don't think so. I wonder if this is why we have trouble sitting quietly in a room alone. This underlying shame becomes unavoidable.

Pascal goes on to say,

> Nothing is so insufferable to man as to be completely at rest, without passions, without business, without diversion, without study. He then feels his nothingness, his forlornness, his insufficiency, his dependence, his weakness, his emptiness.

> There will immediately arise from the depth of his heart wea-
> riness, gloom, sadness, fretfulness, vexation, despair.

Yep. I can relate to all those.

Without what Pascal refers to as diversion, the pain in our lives becomes difficult to conceal. The emotions we've been avoiding become inescapable. We see our loneliness, our disconnection, our insecurity, our inferiority, our worry. These are our weeds. I've heard St. Teresa of Ávila quoted as saying that we must sit in them—with God. I love that phrase. We must sit in our weeds with God. But I hate to do it. It is much easier said than done. I like to ignore them, or mow over them and hope they won't grow back.

But it is only in the stillness that we are able to receive the gladness. Because when we pause and we cease striving, our gaze widens and suddenly we realize that God is near. It can be almost startling.

I remember a roommate of mine had a mannequin. I don't even know where it came from. But every once in a while, he would move it to a different location in our house. And whenever I noticed its new location, I'd practically have a heart attack. I'd catch a glimpse of it out of my peripheral vision and suddenly realize "someone" was in the room with me.

Similarly, I am still often caught off guard when I discover the nearness of God. Usually when God speaks, I'm not even listening. He has to break in and interrupt me for me to hear. Usually, when I get a word from God, it is followed by the humbling realization that he has been speaking it over and over for quite a while.

But when I do hear, I'm learning to remain in that place where God is. It is always vulnerable and demands more truthfulness than I'm comfortable with. I am confronted by the fact that I'm not in control, nor am I able to hide from God. He is always here. And yet it is only in this place of vulnerability and surrender that I can truly taste and see the goodness of God. That it isn't just there for me when I'm strong. That it doesn't withdraw from me when I feel weak and afraid. It is only in this place of transparency that I am able to fully experience the steadfast love of God.

Psalm 34:8 says,

Taste and see that the LORD is good;
   blessed is the one who takes refuge in him.

When I experience God's love at such a vulnerable heart level, my fear dissipates. All the pressure and anxiety of having to perform, to be on, to not disappoint, feels small. I am able to sit in that broken place and receive God's approval. The reality that I'm not just loved, but liked. Not for my gifts, but for my heart. And that love truly is unconditional. It is like a mighty river.

Henri Nouwen writes, "Love casts out fear, and how powerful are we when we are free from fear!" (*Love, Henri*). That is exactly how it feels. Powerful! But it isn't my power. And yet it is within me. And it is just enough for what is being asked of me.

There is a wonderful section in Proverbs where Solomon asks God for two things. The first, that he would be honest. And second, that God would only give him enough food for today. He goes on to explain that if God doesn't give him enough, he will be tempted to steal, and that likewise, if God gives him too much, he is afraid he will forget about God. Wisdom asks for just enough.

And I feel like this is true for my heart as well. God has given me just enough for the tasks to which I'm called. And just enough really means enough to allow me to be generous with my heart. To give of myself without worrying about it running out. Because all that worry and anxiety just burns up my emotional fuel so rapidly. God hasn't given me enough strength to allow me to be both afraid and to love. The two work against each other. When I am afraid, my love is quenched. But when I receive God's love, I find a mighty river. And love casts out the fear.

The love of God reminds us of the greater reality that God is near and that we have enough. The reality of this steadfast love destroys my scarcity mentality. It disarms my avarice. It allows me to love sacrificially.

In Laguna Beach, every June we experience a month of fog. It is often referred to as the June gloom. But you hope that by midday it will "burn off." The warmth causes the clouds to break up. Blue sky and sunlight begin poking through, creating holes in the fog blanket. The fog yields and reveals the bright sky that was there all along.

It takes faith to live this way. I prefer to lead with my plan, and give God the option of showing up. But his way, God's showing up, is plan A. And there really isn't a plan B. My part is to simply stay close to the river.

Psalm 1 tells us that the person whose

> delight is in the law of the LORD,
>   and who meditates on his law day and night . . .
> is like a tree planted by streams of water,
>   which yields its fruit in season and
> whose leaf does not wither—
>   whatever they do prospers.

Prosperity is the outcome of remaining rooted by the river. The tree thrives. Life is abundant and fruit comes in its proper time. To live in this nurturing place is to cease striving and simply yield. To embrace the simplicity of God with us, weeds and all. And to let the river run its course and to take us where it will.

FOR REFLECTION AND CONVERSATION

1. The river is a powerful symbol of God's gracious refreshment of our souls. It cannot be controlled or contained. Instead it invites us to simply wade in. Is there a place in your life where your soul feels refreshed? What is it like to step into the flow of God's grace? What things keep you from wading in?

2. Why is it so difficult for us to remain still? Why do we resist the quiet of the river? What are the things we choose to divert us from the stillness?

3. What comes to mind when you think of sitting in your weeds with God? What are the weeds? How do you imagine God would respond to them?

4. Psalm 1 tells us that the wise person is like a tree planted by the river. That tree lives in a place of continual nourishment. How can we make the river our home? How can we daily take the time to be still and refreshed? How can we live each day in the place where we will grow and thrive?

16

LEAVING AND RETURNING

WHEN I VISIT ST. ANDREW'S ABBEY, my favorite room to stay in is in one of its little secluded hermitages named Mt. Carmel. It's perched higher than others with a view of the beautiful, rustling, fall leaves, and the quiet, still pond. The silence is interrupted only by the gaggle of noisy ducks when they encounter a stranger with bread, or the bells signaling the hours of prayer.

It is a place I've returned to again and again. So much so that the times are beginning to blend into one another. There is a pattern forming over time of intentionally disengaging and reengaging. Of detaching, and then reattaching. And I'm realizing now that this is how we grow. That detachment isn't detachment per se, but instead is a part of the movement. Like a dance step. It is the slow step before the two quick steps.

I've grown to love the scientist-turned-philosopher Michael Polanyi. He writes about knowledge as a necessarily personal journey. All knowledge, even mathematics and science, requires an element of artistic inspiration. Because true knowledge is mastery, and it is only perfected through time, experience, and effort.

Polanyi sees learning and growth as a movement or dance between two points. He labels these two points *proximal* and *distal*.

You can think of them as near and far. These two poles, in order for knowledge to grow, must be traveled between. It is a necessary leaving and returning. It is in this movement that we grow. We experience knowledge that is beyond our ability to speak of. We encounter what lies beyond ourselves.

You can think of the proximal and distal like opposite ends of a blind person's cane. The distal end is the point that has contact with the world around us. The distal is the place where our perceptions touch reality. As we bump into objects with the cane, we feel the objects themselves. Except we don't. In actuality, we are experiencing the opposite end of the cane on the palm of our hands, the proximal end. It is only through the interpretation of these impulses that we are able to encounter what lies beyond us. Only through a necessary element of translation do we have direct contact with the outside world. We do feel the world, even though we are only indirectly touching it.

But have you ever seen a blind person navigating smoothly through our chaotic world? It is incredible to watch. Over time, they become shockingly adept at piloting through the complex traffic of people, objects, and moving vehicles. The cane has become part of them. It is almost as if they can see. Through practice and deep reflection, the world becomes perceptible. The translation happens immediately and without thought.

But it takes hours of experience to master this kind of knowledge. It takes effort to begin to connect the proximal with the distal. But this is how we grow. Through time, these two poles begin to blend into one. The cane disappears, and the blind person can almost see their surroundings.

We go through life with a similar sort of pattern of knowledge. We are constantly interpreting and translating, until our brains will do it automatically for us. Our minds jump to what we expect and our brains fill in the missing pieces. Pretty soon, what required intentionality is now happening in a rote response. Our minds react apart from our will. We eventually lose sight of the proximal, and live completely in the distal.

But further growth requires us to leave this place of familiarity and return to the proximal. Otherwise, we plateau. And over time, we can even forget. We lose our sensitivity. In our lack of attention, our perceptions can atrophy. Familiarity can stunt or even halt our growth. The only way forward is to return back to where we began. To return to the proximal with new senses.

To help us understand this return home, Polanyi uses the metaphor of a pianist. The proximal knowledge, for the piano player, is the practice of scales. It is the memorization of the notes on the page. It is the redundancy and muscle memory necessary to play more and more complex pieces. A pianist is never finished practicing. It is a necessary part of the rhythm. They must return again and again to their scales.

And yet, to truly play a piano, we cannot think of our hands, our fingers, the notes on the page, or the keys themselves. To play, we must leave all of that cognitive thinking to our subconscious. We must forget about them. Only then can we become lost in the music. Only then can we just play.

This difference between the distal and the proximal is awkwardly seen in moments of stage fright, where thinking jars us out of the music and into the proximal focus on our fingers. Has this ever happened to you? It has happened to me plenty of times. A learned piece that we can play effortlessly all of a sudden turns into gibberish. The dance has been interrupted by focusing on the notes themselves and suddenly we've lost our ability to play.

A true master is intentional about practicing. More than simply playing, they spend time in the mechanics, perfecting technique, and going over the difficult places again and again. Mastery happens when our selves melt away and we find something larger than us emerge in process. This type of "playing" is the mastery of the distal end of our knowledge. It is the goal itself. And yet neither the proximal nor the distal are places for us to remain exclusively. If we intend to grow, we must move. We must leave the familiar. We must return home.

And sometimes, this movement can be humbling. How easy it is to neglect the tedious work that proximal knowledge requires. It shows us where we've become sloppy. Practicing scales can be boring and tedious. Most of the time I'd rather just play and not worry about the need to improve.

Recently, I was reminded of this on a surf trip where I surfed the biggest waves of my life. Huge, double overhead waves at a surf spot in Mexico, Rio Nexpa. The surf was perfect. An excellent day. Our surf guide, Juan, couldn't believe how lucky we were. We had the trip planned for months and had traveled all the way to southern Mexico just in time for a huge swell.

The night before, I was restless, listening to the booming surf outside the window of the villa where my friends and I were staying. How big was it? Did I bring the right boards? I found myself praying, *Please God, don't let me drown out there!*

The next morning, we woke at the crack of dawn. We nervously changed and waxed our boards, grabbing leashes, applying sunscreen, and peering out cautiously as the waves rolled in, one after the other, like corduroy all the way to the horizon. Man, did they look big!

I remember paddling out and staying glued to our guide. When he jumped into the water, I was right next to him. As he duck-dived through each wave, so did I. This guy knew this place and I didn't. I wasn't about to leave his side.

I made it outside with a little difficulty, but one of our group got picked off and was swept by the current way down the beach. Eventually he made it back out to us, but by then he was totally exhausted.

I still remember dropping into my first wave, a huge closeout that erupted all around me. As I got to the bottom of the wave I got pitched over the front of my board. When I hit the water, it was like getting thrown out of a moving car. I couldn't believe how fast I was going. I actually skipped on the water before penetrating.

But as I shook my head, the ringing in my ears faded, and I paddled back out for another one. As a set started to roll in, another surf guide, Frederico, shouted for me to go. I paddled with everything I had and pushed over the lip. The wave felt enormous. As I dropped down the face, I glanced up to see where the lip was breaking. I had to crane my head back. I had never been on a wave that big. It was massive. As it stood up in front of me, it took everything mentally for me not to pull out of the wave early. If I didn't make it, I was going to get destroyed.

The wave rose higher and higher above me. I grabbed the rail for stability and shot out in front of the crashing white wash, banking up the face and out the back of the wave. I let out the biggest shout. As I paddled back out to the lineup, I had the hugest grin from ear to ear. My friend Chuck smiled and said, "You got a good one!" My face said it all.

Afterward, I found out that a local kid, Jerry, had a camera and filmed the whole session. I couldn't wait to see the footage. We sat back in the villa that night and watched clip after clip. There were so many great surfers out there. I watched as they elegantly linked their turns, sharp off the top and then fading back in the pocket. Smooth and graceful. There is something so artistic about surfing.

And then I recognized my board. Someone said, "Hey, there's the pastor." As I watched the wave pop up on video, I'm not going to lie, I was a little disappointed. Certainly it was big, but not quite as big as I thought it was. As I dropped in, I could see the caution in my turns. I didn't want to fall, and it showed. I played it safe. As I grabbed the rail and headed for the exit, I could now see that I should've cut back. I wasn't in the pocket. I wasn't surfing the wave to its potential.

Granted, it was the first day. But watching yourself like that can be a very humbling experience. The reality doesn't match the embellished recollection. As another wave of mine popped up on the screen, I was tempted to look away. I didn't want the memory tainted. I preferred my version of the story.

But another part of me fought back. Watch, even if it makes you perspire with humility. Because the truth can set you free. Seeing ourselves like that is painfully revealing, but it is necessary for growth. You'll never progress without it.

The next day the waves were even bigger, but it didn't slow me down. I became more conscious of my turns. I stayed further back on the wave. I pushed myself to come all the way through my cut backs. Because I knew that tonight I'd be staring at that same screen. And I didn't care if I looked better or worse than anyone else. I just wanted. To improve. To grow. Because deep down, that experience is richer. It is one thing to surf well in your mind. Quite another to have it live up to that on film.

This is the invitation of Polanyi's view of personal knowledge. To become an artist, or at least to move in that direction. But progression requires more than the thrills and joys of surfing. It requires uncomfortable scrutiny. It requires humble courage to be seen. And to truly see ourselves. And sometimes that only comes when we take a step back. In this case, the camera provides us with a broader picture of reality.

Reality can feel intrusive. It can be offensive. But it is what it is. It is immovable. It doesn't attack or condemn. It doesn't judge. But it does demand of us integrity. It holds us accountable. It challenges our overly sentimental veneers with which we cover over the blemishes in our lives. Our actions speak so much louder than our words.

I want to grow. As a husband, father, pastor, friend. I don't want to hide from my imperfections or timidities. I want to accept them, and to improve. To have the courage to look at reality without flinching. To submit to its authority. And then to press back aggressively. To make my metaphorical carves and cutbacks with more precision and commitment. Not for the sake of the camera or the viewer, but for the sake of truth. To live and grow in the freedom of reality.

But life doesn't give us an outside camera angle. Well, maybe these days it does. In some ways, our whole lives are now being filmed and recorded, though all we are able to see is what's on the outside. But real growth, emotionally, mentally, and spiritually, happens within us. It takes place in the heart. And the only way I know to separate ourselves enough from the distal dance of life is to disengage from it intentionally. Which brings us back to the abbey.

My times of silent retreat have this very effect on me. They force me to look at the video of my heart, and not just the image in my head. Times of silence and contemplation force me to take a hard look and to ask myself what is really going on inside of me. It shows me just how anxious I am. How lukewarm the temperature has become over time. A part of me resists. But the deeper part of me persists. It knows this is what I need.

Because otherwise, all my time can be spent working and performing and never learning. Never growing. I can get so lost in the music that I fail to recognize where I've become sloppy, where I need to mature.

When I retreat to St. Andrews, all of a sudden my heart comes back into view. And I'm often aghast at all the clutter, all the dissonance going on beneath the surface. Back home, I become so focused on all the demands, I completely lose sight of my heart. I do get subtle hints, like anxiety or worry, moments of anger or impatience. They remind me that there is more going on than I'm aware of. But the only way they come back into view is when I am willing to step away and be still.

The silence in Valyermo has become a sort of homecoming. I step outside of myself; I see my heart. I see where it has become empty or cold. I see the feelings of underappreciation, weariness, and even despair, for what they are—a necessary part of the rhythm. Over the years, as I find myself returning again and again to the place of retreat, I am realizing that a depth is taking place. But it requires a shift in vision. It requires a different metric. It is moving in a different way.

The contemplative life is a life of reflection. It requires quiet and seclusion. But it also requires examination. We separate to look closely at our hearts. To see the thing behind the thing.

Polanyi sees this beautiful epistemological dance between the proximal and the distal as the birthplace of artistry and inspiration, not only for the creative arts, but also science and mathematics. He was a contemporary of Einstein and asked him in a letter if his general theory of relativity was scientifically deduced. Einstein responded and told him that the birthplace of the idea was in his imagination, not in the lab, trying to comprehend what it would be like to be an observer traveling at the speed of light. You can almost hear the glee in Polanyi's writing, as if he is exclaiming, "I knew it!"

The value of Polanyi's model is that it provides us a glance behind the curtain of what most of us take for granted and leave unexamined. It isn't just about what we know, but how we know it. And this allows our hearts to grow. And while we may find ourselves in a battle with our flesh until the day we die, that doesn't mean we aren't growing in a direction, improving . . . towards maturity in Christ.

It is happening in our hearts. Always already. The Spirit is at work. God's voice is whispering, beckoning us further up and further in.

When I come to the abbey I stop working. I stop reflecting on my work. And I start reflecting on the one who is always working and always reflecting on his work. I see again the deep insecurity that often disappears like the water I swim in. I see the need for affirmation that ignores all the compliments to focus on the one complaint. I see the scared, intimidated little Jeff, hoping that someone finally notices him, and that so often longs to be seen as special and unique. I see myself in all my frailty. It is often painfully humbling. But I've grown to appreciate the taste of it, like a good, strong cup of black coffee. Give it to me. Because there is freedom on the other side.

It is here in this place of exposure that I begin to hear again and recognize the still, small voice of God. And it is getting easier and easier to hear. Maybe a part of the growth is simply the ability to hear and know the voice of the shepherd. And to be reminded of the fact that I am, and always will be, one of the sheep.

St. Thérèse of Lisieux has become one of my companions as of late. She is called the little flower and is known for living and modeling what she called the "little way." It is both deeply profound and simplistic. It is the way of the child. It is the way of love. And therefore, it is the way of glory and transcendence.

The little way is the way of surrender. And I'm learning that this is the key. That sustainability in the middle place requires not merely vulnerability and humility, but a deep trust in the love of God. Without this trust, the strain is often more than we can bear. And this knowledge that we long for is the same longing our children have for their father's love.

I see this in my own children—the peace that settles on them when they know they are loved. This is our deepest longing. And without it, our inner lives become a tumult of longing and insecurity.

✧ ◆ ✧

One of the monks here at the Abbey has become a dear friend. His name is Father Francis. He is a Benedictine priest and lives at St. Andrew's Abbey in Valyermo. There is a deep sense of calm that rests on him. It comes out in the way he speaks. It underlies his responses, even when addressing subjects of tension or concern. There is a lack of defensiveness, even when handling delicate or controversial matters of faith. And when responding to potential areas of confusion or doubt, his response is almost whimsical. There is a lightness to him. A playfulness. A deep sense of joy.

Benedictines deeply value community, counsel, and respect for all persons. They live each day in the practice of hospitality. Often they stand at the door to the sanctuary and greet each person entering with the phrase, "Thank God you've come."

Francis has lived at Valyermo for over forty years. He came when he was nineteen and he'll one day be buried in the cemetery at the top of their hill. I love that spot. It is one of the most quiet places on earth. It is sacred ground. Walking among the gravestones you feel the stability of the ones who have remained, who have grown deep roots.

True peace takes years and years to cultivate. Edwin Friedman refers to it as nonanxious presence. I love that! And the prerequisite for this type of presence is self-differentiation, or in simpler terms, knowing oneself. Who you are. Who you aren't.

Whenever I travel to the abbey I am usually wrestling with one or the other. Who am I? Who am I not? Two sides of the same coin. What is my identity? My identity in Christ? What is my true vocation? My true self? Where am I hiding? What are my façades?

Self-discovery is powerful and meaningful, and often humbling. It makes us vulnerable. It exposes our hearts. My deepest longing is to be able to receive the love of God in that place of vulnerability, without pretense or self-protection. I have a long way to go.

But there has been a consistent voice for the last several years when I stay at the abbey. I'll be eating breakfast in silence. Quiet and still. Slowly waking up. Preparing for the day ahead. And I'll hear the voice behind me whisper, "I know you."

And I turn around, and there's Father Francis. Full of such grace and peace. A heart warm, like a fire. Nonanxious presence. I can't help but want to draw close. To warm my own heart.

That phrase gets me every time. It touches a deep longing. My heart leaps. There is such tenderness in the words. When he says it, I hear the whisper of God's voice. And my own heart opens just a little bit more. To be known is so powerful. It is such a vulnerable gift.

Living in that place takes faith. I experience this peace only for brief moments. But slowly it is starting to stick. I'm beginning to speak more honestly. To stand a bit straighter. To release worry and self-criticism. To allow myself to just be who God made me to be. That is true self-differentiation.

This time was no different. As I entered the common room and stood near the large fireplace my friend entered the room. I walked over and gave him a warm embrace. He held me tight and whispered, "I know you."

You have searched me, LORD,
    and you know me.
You know when I sit and when I rise;
    you perceive my thoughts from afar.
You discern my going out and my lying down;
    you are familiar with all my ways.
Before a word is on my tongue
    you, LORD, know it completely.
You hem me in behind and before,
    and you lay your hand upon me.
Such knowledge is too wonderful for me,
    too lofty for me to attain. (Psalm 139:1-6)

FOR REFLECTION AND CONVERSATION

1. Where do you go to be still and to assess the state of your own heart?

2. Is it difficult for you to be still or is it something you enjoy? If it's difficult, what things keep you from making this a regular practice?

3. How is your heart today? If there were a gauge, where would you be at emotionally, physically, spiritually? What can you do to get refilled and renewed?

4. When God speaks to you in that place of stillness, what does he say? What does it feel like to be known? How does this piece of personal knowledge help us to grow?

17

DISCOVERING JOY

I love to read letters. In today's world, letter-writing has become a lost art. But reading the letters of C. S. Lewis, Henri Nouwen, or Flannery O'Connor gives a window behind the scenes. Letters are personal and intimate and give us a deeper and more vulnerable glimpse into the soul of the writer.

I've been reading through Henri Nouwen's letters and continue to love him more and more as I listen to and glean from his tender heart. His correspondence is always filled with such intimacy and humility. One letter in particular stood out to me recently. It was written to someone who had just finished reading his *Genesee Diary*, his journal from his one year stay at the monastery. The writer was saddened that Henri hadn't come away from the time with more of a lasting change. Henri responds by saying,

> I can very well understand that you felt disappointed with the conclusion and often I wished I could have written something else, but I felt I had to be honest and tell the whole truth. Now when I look back at those times, I think that many changes have taken place but maybe not the changes I had hoped for.
>
> The mystery of God's grace is that He often changes us in ways that we were not planning on and that sometimes we do not have eyes to see or ears to hear these changes in ourselves. I deeply believe that God is always active in us and always molding us into new people.

I resonate with this passage so much. I completely agree that God is always molding us. And I also agree that it can feel like God is working on areas we'd prefer be left alone, and that he's neglecting the concerns that feel like the more pressing issues. At times I'm baffled by God's agenda. Sometimes frustrated by it. Occasionally just flat out angered by it.

Sometimes, when I consider the trajectory of my life, I am a bit dismayed that my victories are not more permanent. I often find myself back at the beginning, wishing that all the work I've done had pushed me further than it has. I still find my mind plagued by insecurities. I still long to be adored. I continue to envy the apparent normalcy of others' lives and view myself as deeply flawed.

But I'm learning that these weaknesses are not accidental and are intimately a part of my story. They represent my signature sins. This is the place where I do battle. And victory is not their elimination, but instead a steady and often subtle growth toward deeper character. Toward what Paul calls maturity in Christ.

This battle is, and always will be, where my real work is done. And it happens in the depths of my soul. Because that is what God is after all along. My heart. Which is why God is continually leading me back into the wilderness. This is the place where my heart is tested. It is where I see my weakness exposed and my utter dependency revealed.

Jesus was no stranger to the wilderness. After he was baptized, we are told that the Spirit led him (or sent him as Mark's Gospel suggests) into the wilderness. It is the place of barrenness. Jesus, without food, is harassed after forty days by the devil. It is a time of deep testing. The fragility of Jesus' humanity is exposed.

Often we fail to see the fragility in Christ. It can almost seem as if the testing and temptation of Jesus is a mere formality. We all know that God cannot sin, right? So basically he is just going through the motions.

But I believe that this is a tragic mistake. Think about Jesus in the Garden of Gethsemane on the night when he is betrayed. He is in torment over the cross. His forehead is bleeding through his pores with strain, as he pleads to the Father to take this cup from him. There has to be another way!

I find such comfort in this wrestling. It takes every bit of his heart to surrender to the plans and purposes of his Father. "Not my will but yours be done." Some have said that *this* was the triumphal moment of Jesus' victory. All the rest of the journey to the cross was simply resolve on Jesus' part. The battle of wills had been won and the victory was his surrender. All that remained was to endure the cross.

Similarly, in the desert, Jesus is going to respond to the temptations of the devil by simple submission to the authority and power of the Father. Jesus refuses to act independently of God. He accepts and trusts God's plan, though it may very well contradict his own.

And God's plans usually do contradict something in us. The part that desperately wants to fit in somewhere. To belong. To know where I'm going.

C. S. Lewis talks about this in *Mere Christianity* with his metaphor (actually George McDonald's metaphor) of our lives being a living house in the midst of renovation. We are fine as long as God is doing maintenance on the plumbing or electrical. But when he starts knocking down walls to rooms we had assumed were finished, we start to realize that maybe our blueprints and his are dramatically different. Lewis says,

> The explanation is that He is building quite a different house from the one you thought of—throwing out a new wing here, putting on an extra floor there, running up towers, making courtyards. You thought you were being made into a decent little cottage: but He is building a palace. He intends to come and live in it Himself.

When I think of the home I would like God to build, it is usually smaller and more comfortable than God's plan. His version is often both bigger and smaller than I would prefer. His version costs so much of my ego. All of it, in fact.

When I draw up blueprints for my life, they are always, in some way, geared towards the praise and applause of others. I want to build a life that is impressive. To be seen as brilliant. To have my gifts and talents prominently on display. This world in which I am the center is the world God is inviting me out of.

God's version, instead, focuses on my heart. And although this place is precious to me, I find that I have so little real understanding of it. To find this place requires obedience and surrender. God knows me so much better than I know myself.

I realized this when I went with a group from my church to hear a "prophet" share at a nearby church. We had each sent him our first names and he had prayed over them to see if God had a word of knowledge to give. By now, I'm sure you realize that this brought up in me a certain degree of caution and even suspicion. This isn't my scene. And yet I continue to find a door in my heart open to the more charismatic streams. Sometimes my longings win out over my self-protective dogmas.

As the man spoke, he eventually came to me. And this is what he said: "Joyous Jeff—you're stronger than what you know. There's someone you've underestimated and it's Jeff. And it's time for you to know that you're a king and that you rule with a lot of authority. . . . You'll do it in a gentle way. There are ones that really need to hear and how you help unlock them in the days to come. You have a symphony of hope . . . reformers that are walking with you."

As I read those words again, my heart aches. Joyous Jeff. That is who I want to be. And so rarely do I feel worthy of that name. But it rings true. So true. And all my other names for myself feel so trivial in comparison. Brilliant Jeff. Insightful Jeff. Even Wise Jeff. All those names have this perfect blend of both my will and God's will combined. And that never seems to work. My ego can never be appeased.

But Joyous Jeff . . . there is no way I can become that on my own. I long for it, but I cannot make it so. Instead I must yield to the work God is doing. I cannot muster up the joy. It has to flow through me. And that requires a heart that is pure and free.

And I have so much further to go. But I'm starting to slowly see the fruit. And so are others. They sheepishly tell me that they see how much I'm growing. And I realize that with that comes the reality that my past weaknesses have been far more apparent than I want to admit. But also, that they are watching my heart change. That I'm gradually becoming more free. Becoming more myself.

It reminds me of Merton's quote in *New Seeds of Contemplation*: "For me to be a saint means to be myself. Therefore the problem of sanctity and salvation is in fact the problem of finding out who I am and of discovering my true self."

That is the person that God is always molding. And he's doing more than growing my true self. He's also shaping my desires along with it. Helping me to see how bankrupt my small visions of self-centered glory are compared to the freedom of simply being who he has made me to be.

The other day I got a glimpse into my own growth. I was performing a wedding for a dear friend. It was her second marriage and also his. Both were coming out of incredibly dysfunctional past relationships, and were a bit in shock at just how good this new relationship was. All of us there felt such a sense of redemption for these two. They deserved each other, in the very best sense. It was beautiful to watch and an honor to perform.

But afterwards several people came up and gave me the very same compliment. They said how much they loved the service and the words I shared and all that, but what caught my attention was that when they spoke of the power behind the service, they all pointed to a deep feeling of joy that I conveyed.

And that felt right. There was a purity to the way my heart received that compliment. I simply felt grateful. Grateful of the continuing work that God was doing. And a relief that we were doing this according to his plan, and not my own. The compliment of joy captures both the fullness of glory and the meekness of humility. And I realized that this is what my heart longed for above all else.

And that feels like growth. There is nothing spectacular about being filled with joy, and yet it is glorious. Joyous Jeff. How I want to be that.

So I will continue to do battle with my insecurity and with my pride. I will continue to go into the wilderness, because that is where the battle for my freedom lies. I will continue to press into my insecurities and feel their pain, because the healing I've experienced there has given me hope.

Enjoying the wilderness is an acquired taste. Like the goodness of strong coffee or the beautiful complexity of wine. It takes work to understand the true value of the desert. But freedom, as with anything of true value, requires discipline and perseverance. Because most of the time we are resisting this place of truth and honesty. In the wilderness, the truth shines most brightly.

Because the stark truth of the wilderness isn't diminished by social acceptance or our self-rationalization. Those things are gone. The wilderness demands honesty, almost brutal honesty. As Edward Abbey says, "Better a cruel truth than a comfortable delusion." And he's right. In the wilderness our false selves are exposed for what they truly are. False idols.

✧ ✦ ✧

I have grown through this process, and yet part of that growth is watching the line on the horizon be pushed further and further away. God is asking more of me than I had previously imagined. And yet, in that fact lies such a rich hope. God holds this reality up to me and invites me into glory. There is always more to learn.

"You are a king and you rule with a lot of authority, but you'll do it in a gentle way." I cling to that promise.

Thérèse of Lisieux, in *The Story of a Soul*, says, "So it is not intellect or talents that Jesus has come upon earth to seek. He became the Flower of the fields solely to show us how He loves simplicity. . . . What a privilege to be called to so high a mission! . . . But to respond to it how simple one must remain."

Our mission is both high and simple. All of our missions are. Each of us is on a unique path, with unique inner battles to be fought and intimate self-discovery to be made. And we need each other to have the courage to enter into this place.

Victor Frankl writes in *Man's Search for Meaning*, "Everyone has his own specific vocation or mission in life; everyone must carry out a concrete assignment that demands fulfillment. Therein he cannot be replaced, nor can his life be repeated; thus, everyone's task is unique as his specific opportunity to implement it."

Each of our journeys is unique, and yet the themes and patterns are ubiquitous. All of us are being led on a path of self-denial and pushed towards glory. All of us are offered a story that is both smaller and larger than we'd prefer. But the fruit of this path we take is freedom and salvation for our heart. It is the greatest gift we can give to each other, to God, and ultimately, to ourselves.

FOR REFLECTION AND CONVERSATION

1. Are you aware of where God is at work renovating your heart? How do you feel about it? Do you agree with the changes God wants to make?

2. I was surprised to find God calling out the joy in me. Is there a time when God called something deeper out in you? Were you surprised by what it was?

3. Joy was both smaller and larger than what I had imagined for myself. Can you relate? How is God calling your true heart to become greater? What will this cost?

AFTERWORD

THESE PAST FEW WEEKS HAVE BEEN HUMBLING. I find myself confronted once again with new levels of insecurity within myself. New and yet familiar. Do you remember that thing I was waiting for? Well . . . it fell apart in disappointment. My heart was broken. Not by the rejection itself, but by the frustration of having put my heart out there only to have my hopes dashed. Hope is so dangerous and risky. But I felt like I was being obedient to take the risk. I had stepped out in faith. But if that is true, then maybe the heartbreak itself was the point. And it was intentional.

The work of heart transformation is like peeling away layers of an onion. And this can be a painful process. And the work is never-ending. The wounds run so deep. And so the work will always continue. I say this to remind myself that I will never be finished. Not in this lifetime.

The one constant thing in this life is change. The warmth of summer fades. The long days will begin to shorten. The temperatures will start to cool. And we'll find ourselves gearing up for the fall once again. For the next stage of the journey. And we'll remind ourselves that all of this is worth it. That the deep heart work of transformation is what gives life its meaning and beauty. And that our roots continue to deepen.

There is a seasonal dance we are all swept up in. We are all participants, willingly or unwillingly. But we can choose how we respond.

We can resist the movement, or we can yield to it. To be present in it. And to trust the leadings of God. The nudges and the twirls.

And above all, we are invited to savor it for all its beauty and the depth and meaning that it provides. This is where hope resides. This is how we grow.

But if we aren't careful, the seasons can begin to blur. Progress gets overlooked in the familiar. We lose sight of tangible measurements. And we start to lose sight of where we're going and how far we've come.

Because when we grow, especially later in life, there are very few accolades. No more graduation ceremonies or pomp and circumstance. In fact, growth is more like the shrug of our shoulders. What seemed, at one time, an overwhelming burden or anxiety, suddenly seems small and inconsequential. The tendency is to look back at ourselves with pity. "What was I so afraid of?"

And what we miss is the monumental leap forward that has taken place. Those past concerns feel small because our hearts have enlarged. And the shrug isn't indifference. It is freedom. What once had a hold on us no longer does. We can see it with new eyes.

And this growth is glory. We are stepping more into who we are. Into our vocation. Into the true self. It is glorious. But it is also humble. The ego is losing its grip. We are being transformed.

When this happens, my spiritual director, Lynn, will have us pause. Partly because I'm always on to the next thing. But mostly to give thanks. This is the deep work of God. It is sacred and holy.

My hope for you is that this book has invited you to look at your own heart. Where you've been. Where you find yourself today. But also to shape how you look ahead. That the questions and reflections at the end of each chapter would become themes and useful tools throughout the seasons of your life. That the pauses to examine your heart would become a necessary and cherished part of your rhythm. And that participating in the deep, slow work of God would become one of the intimate desires of your heart.

And that as you grow through the seasons, that you'd notice the growth. That you would pause and savor. And that your heart would experience the freedom of being you.

ACKNOWLEDGMENTS

WHEN MY DEAR FRIEND Mark Metherell first suggested I write a book, I knew it was less a request and more a command. But the request wasn't merely out of amusement or curiosity. His end goal was always that we would change the world. From time to time he would hold up his hands, almost as if in prayer, slowly tapping his fingers together, and ask me, ever so slyly, "So how's the book coming?"

Mark was a Navy Seal and several years later he lost his life fighting overseas in Iraq. I still miss him so much. He continues to be the depiction to me of nobility, integrity, poetry, and whimsy, all wrapped in one. I have never met anyone else like him.

Here it is, my friend. For what it's worth. Thank you for believing in me and this project. Maybe, just maybe, it'll push back the darkness a bit and shine forth some much needed light.

And thank you for the book group you "asked" me to lead that continues on to this day. The roster has changed quite a bit over the last decade, but the spirit of liveliness, curiosity, and a dash or two of sarcasm still remains. Thank you to Chuck, and Tom, Drew, Charlie, Dave Burchi, Phil, Steve, Terry, and Kate, and anyone else who has slogged through one of the countless books we've read at that wonderful intersection between philosophy, theology, science, history, and the arts.

Thank you to those who have constantly inspired and pushed me beyond my procrastinating and self-limiting beliefs. To J. P. Moreland and Len Sweet, who pushed me to think deeper and further than I ever would. To Rob Bell who continues to affirm that originality is simply for you to say it in your own words, and that God always insists on our greatness. And for my wonderful faculty team at CFDM, Care Crawford, Steve Summerell, and, of course, Lynn Ziegenfuss, who also serves as my spiritual director and Jedi master. Thank you all for the wonderful investment you've made in me.

Thank you to my delightful Little Church by the Sea in Laguna Beach, and to the remarkably gifted team of pastors and leaders I am so privileged to work with. Thank you to Jay, and Chris, and Toby, and Sam, and Kelly and Greg. I am so blessed to get to do life and ministry with you all!

Thank you to all of you that helped form this book through countless conversations and moments of much-needed encouragement. To Gabe Sullivan, Dave Tosti, Melanie Wolf, Bret Fleming, Terry and Regina Jacobson, Paul Wolfe, Bret Reed, Billy Tarka, Lars Rood, Brad Coleman, the whole Papadopulos clan, my sisters, Susan and Carolyn, and so many more.

And of course Mom and Dad. Thank you for giving me something so solid to begin with and the encouragement as well to question and, at times, push against.

And thank you especially to the wonderful Cathleen Falsani, for pushing me through every single one of the hurdles involved in publishing a book, from the proposal, to finding my brilliant agent, Chris Ferebee, and the wonderful introduction to Cindy Bunch and her phenomenal team at IVP. What a gift you all are to me!

And lastly, thank you to my delightful children and beloved wife. To Gabe, my thoughtful, deep, drummer/surfer/philosopher. To Mia, my brilliant, artistic, scientific mastermind. To Lila, with her enormous heart, rocking voice, and contagious zeal for life. And to Patty, who I can't live without. My best friend, deepest love, most trusted critic, faithful coach, and most enduring fan. Yours is the only opinion that truly matters to me. I love you like crazy.

‡formatio

Formatio books from InterVarsity Press follow the rich tradition of the church in the journey of spiritual formation. These books are not merely about being informed, but about being transformed by Christ and conformed to his image. Formatio stands in InterVarsity Press's evangelical publishing tradition by integrating God's Word with spiritual practice and by prompting readers to move from inward change to outward witness. InterVarsity Press uses the chambered nautilus for Formatio, a symbol of spiritual formation because of its continual spiral journey outward as it moves from its center. We believe that each of us is made with a deep desire to be in God's presence. Formatio books help us to fulfill our deepest desires and to become our true selves in light of God's grace.